Special Needs Assessment
Specific Learning Difficulties

SNAP

SNAP-SpLD 4–16

User's Handbook

Charles Weedon,
Gavin Reid and
Kate Ruttle

RS ASSESSMENT
FROM HODDER EDUCATION

Acknowledgements

The authors of SNAP-SpLD would like to thank the staff and pupils of Moorfoot Primary School, Midlothian, specifically Carla Jamieson, for their help and assistance.

We would also like to thank the following schools for participating in trialling the Diagnostic Probe content:
Al Salaam Private School; Worle Village Primary School; Paradykes Primary School; Edgebury Primary; Stonehill Primary; Saint Benedict Catholic Voluntary Academy; Rodborough School; Northallerton School & 6th Form College; Focus School - Linton Park Campus; Forest Academy; West Rise School Sussex; Trinity Academy London; Hotham Primary School; Walliscote Primary School; Tower Road Academy; Sacred Heart RC Primary; Haydock English Martyrs Primary School; Ickleford Primary School; Garden Fields JMI School; St Clement and St James CE Primary School; Loretto School; Bristol Brunel Academy; Droylsden Academy; Saint Felix School; British School of Brussels.

Orders: please contact Hachette UK Distribution, Hely Hutchinson Centre, Milton Road, Didcot, Oxfordshire, OX11 7HH. Telephone: (44) 01235 400555. Email: primary@hachette.co.uk.

Lines are open from 9 a.m. to 5 p.m., Monday to Friday, with a 24-hour message answering service. Visit our website at www.rsassessment.com for details of other assessment publications.

Online support and queries. Email: onlinesupport@rsassessment.com

ISBN: 978 1 5104 0011 5

First published in 2018 by
RS Assessment from Hodder Education, part of the Hodder Education Group
An Hachette UK Company
Carmelite House
50 Victoria Embankment
London EC4Y 0DZ

www.rsassessment.com

Impression number 10 9 8 7 6 5

Year 2022 2021 2020

Authors: Charles Weedon, Gavin Reid and Kate Ruttle
Publishers: Tracey Riseborough and Sarah Minty
Designer: Steve Pargeter

Cover design: Steve Pargeter
Typeset in: India
Printed in: the U.K.
A catalogue record for this title is available from the British Library.

Contents

1 Introduction to SNAP-SpLD

What is SNAP-SpLD?

The Special Needs Assessment Profile-Specific Learning Difficulties (SNAP-SpLD) is an online assessment tool that enables schools to identify likely special educational needs (SENs) or specific learning difficulties (SpLDs) in pupils aged 4–16 years. SNAP-SpLD is a wide-angle in-depth diagnostic resource in that it scans the widest realistic range of SpLDs and conditions at the same time as probing as deeply as possible to identify their underlying bases. It can be used with any pupil and allows schools and parents to take the first steps towards an understanding that would otherwise require significant and expensive multi-agency input.

SNAP-SpLD is made up of several different components:

- **Pupil Assess**ment Questionnaire is completed by teaching staff in school who know the pupil best.
- Diagnostic Probes – eight short tests (two of them in two parts), which provide additional quantitative evidence about the pupil and his or her abilities.
- Information from the Family Questionnaire draws on the perceptions of the parents/carers to profile the child or young person in his or her home environment.
- What I Feel Questionnaire allows for analysis of the pupil's own perceptions about his or her self-esteem, both educationally and socially.
- **Pupil's Voice Record: What's Important to Me?** seeks to capture and present the pupil's own insights and understandings about himself or herself as a learner.

SNAP-SpLD can be used just with the questionnaires so that no actual testing with the pupil is needed or, more usually, some or all of the Diagnostic Probes are used in order to contribute significant further evidence to the results. It takes around 40–45 minutes for younger pupils to complete the probes, while the reading and listening tasks used with older pupils may take longer.

Pupil Assessment Questionnaire

The Pupil Assessment Questionnaire should be completed online by the teacher (or other school personnel) who knows the pupil best. This questionnaire asks the teacher to reflect on what he or she already knows and has observed about the pupil and provides a detailed report on strengths and difficulties via the **Core Profile**.

Most of the 162 questions have a choice of five responses and can be answered very quickly, directly on-screen, for example:

Does s/he seem to have unusually all-absorbing/ obsessive interests?	Never	Rarely	Age appropriate	Often	Always

'Age appropriate' is the baseline – it means that, for this trait or behaviour, this is about what you might expect from most children of the same age. Meaning you really haven't noticed anything in particular about that trait.

For example, for 'Does s/he seem to have unusually all-absorbing/ obsessive interests?', the 'Age appropriate' response would suggest she or he may want to spend all day on the iPad if allowed, or play with Lego for hours at a time, but really not more or less than lots of other children.

If you chose 'Often' then that would suggest that it is maybe that little bit more obvious than in lots of other children; and if it was 'Always' that would mean that this kind of obsessiveness was very noticeable indeed, a lot more obvious than in most children.

If you chose 'Rarely' it would suggest that this child was noticeably less obsessive than most other children; and if you chose 'Never' it would suggest that it was very noticeable that this child never seemed too obsessive about any particular activity.

Information from the Family Questionnaire

This questionnaire should be completed by parents/carers to provide a rounded perspective of the child's abilities. It accesses information that may be diagnostically important in understanding a pupil but which is perhaps more likely to be known of at home rather than at school.

Most of the 38 questions have a choice of five responses, for example:

How good is your child's memory for short-term information (e.g. temporarily remembering phone numbers, e-mail addresses, short shopping lists, etc.)?	Very good	Quite good	Age appropriate	Not very good	Very poor

For some other questions there are just three response options, for example:

Does reading cause your child visual fatigue, headaches or migraines?	No	A little	A lot

Diagnostic Probes

Eight supplementary Diagnostic Probes, or short assessments, are available to add a significant objective element to a process which otherwise draws primarily upon analysing the essentially subjective insights of those who know the pupil best. **Note:** these should only be used with pupils who are seven years or older. The Diagnostic Probes feed into and improve the validity of the pupil's final profile. They explore a range of important skills that have a direct bearing on learning, namely:

- reading and listening for understanding
- phonological awareness and decoding non-words
- spelling
- copying text
- backward memory span
- visual memory
- balancing
- naming pictures.

More information about the Diagnostic Probes is provided in Chapter 3, pages 13–16.

What I Feel Questionnaire

This optional 20-item questionnaire can be completed online or via the printed downloadable PDF, by the pupil being profiled.[1] It allows insight into a pupil's self-image, both socially and as a learner, and provides a potentially valuable

[1] The same questionnaire is also available to users of SNAP-B 5–16.

further understanding of how that pupil functions in the classroom. Self-esteem is included in SNAP-SpLD as an important part of a pupil's profile, but only to offer insight and not to classify it as a SpLD. The pupil's self-esteem is profiled as two substrands: social self-esteem and academic self-esteem. The questions are quite simple but should be read out to younger pupils and discussed if necessary. Again, the questions have a choice of five responses, for example:

I like it when I'm asked questions in class because I quite often know the right answer.	Always	Usually	About average	Only sometimes	Hardly ever

Pupil's Voice Record: What's Important to Me?

Another optional but valuable component, this record allows the pupil's voice to be captured and recorded more informally. Including pupils in their decisions about their diagnosis, care and supported is stipulated in the SEND Code of Practice (DfE, 2015)[2] and is an important part of SEN provision so schools should have clear evidence of how they achieve this.

Using prompts, staff elicit from the pupil an account of his or her preferences and aspirations as a learner, thereby providing an important shared context within which the school, pupil and family may develop their understandings of how the learner may best develop and strengthen.

More information about the Pupil's Voice Record: What's Important to Me? can be found in Chapter 4, pages 17–21.

What does SNAP-SpLD do?

In order for effective learning to happen, many skills need to be deployed simultaneously and automatically. SNAP-SpLD provides a systematic and comprehensive overview of a pupil's SpLDs by identifying his or her relative strengths and difficulties among many different skills (see Figure 1.1 below).

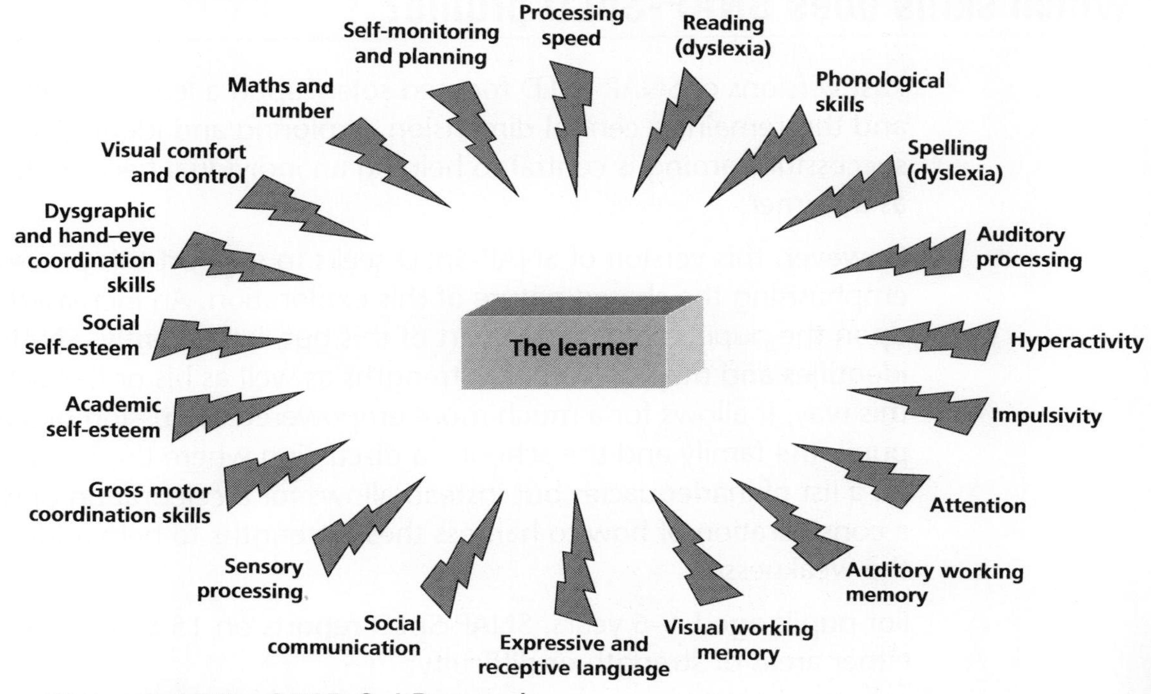

Figure 1.1: The SNAP-SpLD strands

[2] The Code of Practice is applicable in England. Visit https://www.gov.uk/government/publications/send-code-of-practice-0-to-25

Where any or several of these skills are not yet well developed, there may be one or more SpLDs causing a barrier to the pupil's learning. SpLDs are not always well understood so SpLD interventions are often neither as precise nor as effective as they might be. By telling us which of these skills are not yet well developed, SNAP-SpLD allows us to make interventions more precise and effective.

For example, many of us are happy with concepts such as 'dyslexia' when there is an obvious discrepancy between apparent academic potential and current levels of literacy, but arguably this is about as useful as saying someone has a 'fever' when they are hot and sticky and running a temperature. It states the obvious but does not tell us what to do. SNAP-SpLD, however, provides useful information indicating that there is, for example, a mixture of phonological difficulties, some visual stress, poor visual memory and some attentional difficulties. Once this is known, the root causes of the poor literacy may be more effectively addressed.

SNAP-SpLD is not a 'test' – that is, it is not a psychometric instrument. Instead it provides a means to draw together (from family, teachers, SENCO, classroom assistants and the pupil) and organise all that is known about a learner. This is supplemented, where needed, with further information from the Diagnostic Probes. While some of these are quantitative measures, they are not standardised tests as they do not rank and discriminate. Rather they seek to offer an insight into whether there is a problem, whether modest or obvious, with a particular skill, as well as showing where skills are well established. The Core Profile provided by SNAP-SpLD is a description not a diagnosis. Affixing a label implies some kind of certainty about just what causes the difficulty, what it stems from. Diagnosis is a medical term which should be used with caution by educators. Even the most rigorously derived label for a SpLD may still be no more than a description dignified as a diagnosis.

Which skills does SNAP-SpLD profile?

Past versions of SNAP-SpLD focused solely upon a learner's difficulties, and this remains a central dimension. Exploring and identifying barriers to successful learning is central to helping an individual become more successful as a learner.

However, this version of SNAP-SpLD seeks to support this process by emphasising the shared nature of this exploration. An increased emphasis upon the pupil's voice is one part of this but, importantly, SNAP-SpLD now identifies and maps a learner's strengths as well as his or her difficulties. In this way, it allows for a much more empowered discussion between the pupil, the family and the school – a discussion where the central focus is not on a list of inadequacies but instead allows for a celebration of strengths and a consideration of how to harness these strengths to help address or bypass the weaknesses.

For pupils aged 4–6 years, SNAP-SpLD reports on 15 strands, expressed as either areas of strength or difficulty.

For pupils aged 7–16 years, SNAP-SpLD reports on 20 strands, expressed as either areas of strength or difficulty.

How and when to use SNAP-SpLD

SNAP-SpLD is intended principally for use by the class teacher, SENCO / Support for Learning staff, or person with equivalent responsibility, at school or local authority level, including peripatetic advisory teachers. Equally, it may be useful to educational psychologists or health service practitioners involved in assessing or responding to learning difficulties. An experienced teaching assistant may well have an important role in completing the questionnaires and administering the Diagnostic Probes.

At the school level, SNAP-SpLD will have particular value at the point at which a school is considering seeking support from beyond the school for an individual pupil.

Schools tend to use SNAP-SpLD with pupils who:

- are referred for potential SENs
- are not diagnosed with a learning need but are causing concern in the classroom
- have been identified as needing intervention but have not typically responded to intervention
- present with attention issues.

Schools tend to use SNAP-SpLD when:

- teachers or parents have concerns
- teachers need more information/strategies to use with pupils who are experiencing difficulties
- the SENCO is not sure which area of need to focus on.

Schools tend to find SNAP-SpLD useful to:

- obtain a 'fuller picture' of a pupil's overall learning profile
- inform the special education referral process
- form a basis for discussion with parents/carers about possible further support or assessment
- gather data on areas of need
- provide a baseline or an initial profile
- provide information and ideas to both school and home
- show teachers where to focus support
- form the basis for a referral to an educational psychologist, paediatrician, speech and language therapist, etc. The information provided can supplement these professionals' findings in putting together Education, Health and Care (EHC) Plans, formerly known as SEN Statements.

2 SNAP-SpLD reports, feedback and action

Once all the information has been gathered, SNAP-SpLD produces four types of feedback that provide an overview of the strengths and difficulties a pupil is encountering and how these can be addressed both at school and at home.

Overview of the reports and feedback

SNAP-SpLD generates four types of feedback:

- **Core Profile**
- **School Report**
- **Home Report**
- **Information Sheets.**

Together these provide a detailed and wide-ranging picture of the pupil's strengths and difficulties, generating a wealth of information about the pupil, the difficulties he or she is encountering and how these difficulties can be addressed effectively both by his or her teachers and parents/carers. As well as identifying probable barriers to learning, the reports offer an invaluable tool for planning and implementing targeted and personalised interventions to reduce those barriers and for monitoring progress.

Core Profile

The Core Profile draws upon information from the Pupil Assessment Questionnaire, the Diagnostic Probes, the Information from the Family Questionnaire and the What I Feel Questionnaire. Using a graphical format, it shows, for each strand, into which category the pupil's skills appear to be. For most of the skills, these are: Well above average / Above average / Average / Below average / Well below average. See Figure 2.1 on the next page, where the horizontal axis represents the actual average, the 50th percentile.

School Report

Most importantly, SNAP-SpLD suggests what you can *do* about any difficulties identified by the Core Profile. The personalised School Report provides helpful but general tips and advice for managing the pupil's identified difficulties in the classroom. Personal knowledge of the individual pupil will allow a more customised plan to be developed through the inclusion of specific interventions and activities which are provided for each identified difficulty. Relevant interventions and activities can be chosen, and are automatically included in the report, to be implemented at school. The School Report should be shared with all relevant teaching staff.

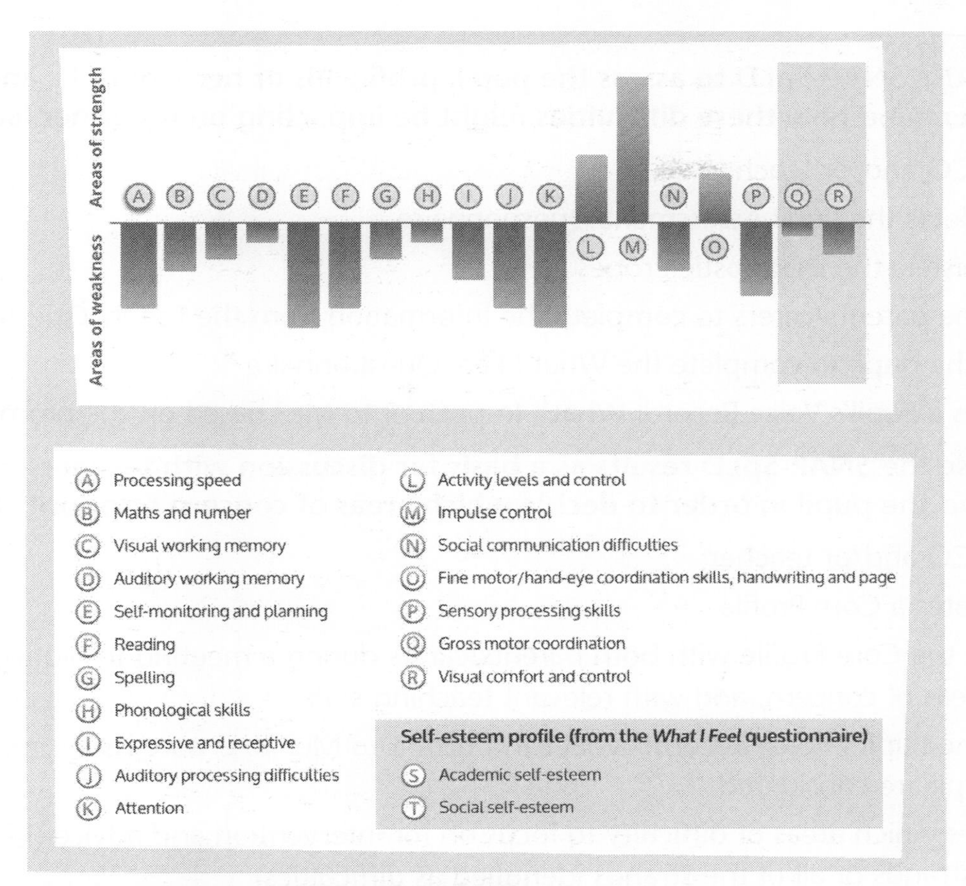

Figure 2.1: Example of a Core Profile

Home Report

The personalised Home Report should be shared with parents/carers to help them gain a better understanding of their child's difficulties. It includes ideas on how to help manage the difficulty at home, as well as activities to try in the home environment. A summary of the interventions being implemented in school is also provided in the Home Report.

Information Sheets

To help both teachers and parents/carers develop a better understanding of the difficulties that appear most prominently on the pupil's Core Profile, Information Sheets are available for each strand (see Figure 2.1). These sheets can be found in the SNAP-SpLD Resources Bank and should be printed out and shared with parents/carers and teachers as needed.

Assess, Plan, Do, Review

SNAP-SpLD has been built to fit around the *Assess, Plan, Do, Review* model as outlined in the SEND Code of Practice (DfE, 2015)[3] using a process in which the SENCO and/or teacher work collaboratively with both the parents/carers and the pupil to plan and evaluate outcomes. SNAP-SpLD allows you to plan and implement targeted and focused interventions that address specific needs and barriers.

[3] The Code of Practice is applicable in England. Visit https://www.gov.uk/government/publications/send-code-of-practice-0-to-25.

ASSESS: Use SNAP-SpLD to assess the pupil, profile his or her strengths and difficulties and understand how these difficulties might be impacting on his or her learning.

The SENCO and/or teacher:

- Completes the Pupil Assessment Questionnaire
- Administers the Diagnostic Probes
- Asks the parents/carers to complete the Information from the Family Questionnaire
- Asks the pupil to complete the What I Feel Questionnaire
- Creates a Pupil's Voice Record: What's Important to Me? based on the prompts provided

PLAN: Use the SNAP-SpLD results as a basis for discussion with teachers, the parents/ carers and the pupil in order to decide which areas of concern to prioritise for action.

The SENCO and/or teacher:

- Generates a Core Profile
- Shares the Core Profile with both parents/carers during a meeting to highlight strengths and areas of concern, and with relevant teaching staff
- Uses the Pupil's Voice Record: What's Important to Me? to ensure issues important to the pupil are considered
- Decides which areas of difficulty to focus on for intervention and advice (i.e. one strand, a few strands or all of the strands identified as difficulties)
- Selects these specific areas and relevant advice / interventions are inserted into the School Report and the Home Report online
- Arranges a date for review or reassessment (up to three assessments can be carried out per pupil)

DO: Use the SNAP-SpLD reports to implement advice and interventions both in school and at home.

The SENCO and/or teacher:

- Generates a School Report to share with all relevant teaching staff – this includes advice on managing the SpLD/s in the classroom and relevant interventions to be implemented
- Generates a Home Report and encourages the parents/carers to implement the activities and advice suggested for managing the identified difficulty at home
- Uses the Information Sheets to provide both parents/carers and teachers/support staff with more detail on the strands that were identified as barriers to learning
- Carefully monitors the progress of the pupil, making notes about any strategies and resources which have been particularly helpful and any improvements that have been made

REVIEW: Reflection on progress made.

The SENCO and/or teacher:

- Uses relevant tests to monitor progress at appropriate intervals; alternatively, progress can be evaluated against any SMART targets set
- Reviews the progress made with both the parents/carers and the pupil at the agreed date
- Repeats the cycle using SNAP-SpLD as the basis for reassessment (you can reassess a pupil as many times as you like, but only three Core Profiles can be compared at one time to track progress)

Figure 2.2: The Assess, Plan, Do, Review model for SNAP-SpLD

3 The Diagnostic Probes

The eight Diagnostic Probes explore nine contributory skill-sets important for effective learning (Probe 1 uses the same material to explore both reading for understanding and listening for understanding). The probes are not essential. SNAP-SpLD can be used effectively without them by using the questionnaires only, or you can pick 'n' mix using whichever probes seem suitable for an individual pupil or that you feel you need. However, the probes do contribute additional objective information to a pupil's final profile, thus enhancing its validity.

The norms have been derived for the 7–16 age range (see Chapter 7) and can only be used with pupils who are 7+.

Overview of each probe

Probe 1A: Reading for Understanding

- **Purpose:** To allow insight into the pupil's reading for understanding.
- **Insight provided:** How effectively can a pupil can understand and take meaning from written prose?
- **Method:** 15 passages are presented, ranging from short and very simple single sentences to extended and quite complex and demanding expository prose. The accompanying questions are multiple-choice and the pupil has to select the correct option from four possible options.
- **Score:** The pupil's score feeds into the 'Reading' strand with a weighting of 20 points.
- This probe can be administered online or offline using the downloadable material provided.

Probe 1B: Listening for Understanding

- **Purpose:** To allow insight into the pupil's listening for understanding.
- **Insight provided:** Comparison of the score achieved when reading independently and the score achieved when listening to the material allows an insight into the extent to which reading may be a barrier to learning. Only the items that were not completed successfully in the reading for understanding task are used here to avoid a practice effect. For competent readers, the two scores would be similar, or perhaps higher for the reading, as the pupil can linger over the text and consider it more carefully. Where a pupil's score is significantly higher for listening, the quality of thinking is reduced by having to read independently, implying a difficulty of a dyslexic nature. The probe therefore explores the extent to which a pupil's understanding of material is limited by having to read the text independently – is it more easily understood if it is heard rather than read?

- **Method:** The administrator reads the passages, the questions and the options aloud, twice. The pupil does not have the passages but does have the questions and options on-screen to avoid working memory overload.
- **Score:** The pupil's score feeds into the 'Expressive and receptive language' strand with a weighting of 20 points.
- This probe can be administered online or offline using the downloadable material provided.

Probes 2A and 2B: Phonological Awareness: Sound Deletion and Non-word Decoding

- **Purpose:** To allow insight into the pupil's ability to discriminate and manipulate the constituent sounds that make up words and to blend these sounds.
- **Insight provided:** Literacy difficulties may stem from a number of different causes or any mixture of those causes including phonological difficulties, visual difficulties, memory difficulties, attentional issues and so on. If a pupil has difficulty at this level of phonological processing, it suggests that any intervention should emphasise phonic decoding and processing.
- **Method:** In part A, the pupil is asked to take an identified sound out of a made-up word. In the part B, the pupil is asked to read some non-words.
- **Score:** The pupil's score feeds into the 'Phonological skills' strand with a weighting of 20 points.
- Probe 2A is administered offline using the downloadable material provided; Probe 2B can be administered online or offline.

Probe 3: Spelling

- **Purpose:** To allow insight into how accurately the pupil can spell age-appropriate words.
- **Insight provided:** To what extent does accurate spelling constitute a strength or a difficulty for this pupil in committing ideas to paper? Where spelling is relatively weak, the pupil's scores in Probes 2 and 6 might suggest how best to intervene. For example, weak spelling with competent visual memory but weak phonological processing suggests a phonically-based intervention, whereas weak spelling with weak visual memory but competent phonological processing suggests that any intervention should emphasise whole-word processing and memory.
- **Method:** The word to be spelled is given, given again in the context of a sentence and then repeated a third time before the pupil writes it on the answer sheet provided.
- **Score:** The pupil's score feeds into the 'Spelling' strand with a weighting of 20 points.
- This probe is administered offline using the downloadable materials provided.

Probe 4: Timed Text Copying

- **Purpose:** To allow insight into the learner's speed and quality of handwriting.
- **Insight provided:** By measuring how many words are copied in 1 minute, this probe explores the extent to which speed and accuracy of handwriting is a strength or a difficulty in committing ideas to paper. Where the speed and quality of writing is obviously incongruent with the pupil's level of ability and likely in itself to constitute a barrier to attainment, then digital alternatives for writing might be indicated.
- **Method:** The pupil is given a short passage for copying, appropriate to his or her age (7–8 years or 9–16 years). The number of words copied in 1 minute is noted. Incorrect copying and legibility are taken into account in scoring.
- **Score:** The pupil's score feeds into the 'Dysgraphic and hand–eye coordination skills, handwriting and page layout' strand with a weighting of 20 points.
- This probe is administered offline using the downloadable materials provided.

Probe 5: Backward Span

- **Purpose:** To allow insight into the pupil's auditory working memory, looking at how much auditory information a pupil can hold in mind while working with it.
- **Insight provided:** This probe indicates the extent to which poor auditory working memory might impact on learning across a wide range of skills including literacy, numeracy, listening skills, following instructions, ability to sustain attention and many more. Working memory is the system that actively holds multiple pieces of transitory information in the mind, where they can be manipulated and processed. A useful analogy is that of a 'cognitive workbench' – a working space (be it a desk, kitchen worktop or a workbench) that is too small and overcrowded and is therefore very frustrating. Things fall off, get mislaid or buried and cannot be located at the moment they are needed, making simple tasks impossibly difficult. Where auditory working memory is relatively weak, cognitive function will easily overload or bottleneck. We have all experienced that sudden rush of anger and frustration when an overload point is reached (e.g. when we are trying to note down what someone is saying when they are going too fast, we simply cannot keep up and they simply won't slow down). Another response is to withdraw, leading to apparent distractibility and inattention.
- **Method:** The pupil is read increasingly long lists of single words and asked to repeat the list backwards.
- **Score:** The pupil's score feeds into the 'Auditory working memory' strand with a weighting of 20 points.
- This probe is administered offline using the downloadable materials provided.

Probe 6: Visual Memory

- **Purpose:** To allow insight into a pupil's visual memory, looking at how much visual information a pupil can hold in mind while working with it.

- **Insight provided:** Weak visual memory can impact very directly on whole-word recognition and retention, affecting both reading and spelling. It can also impact on curriculum areas that make use of diagrams, maps, charts, graphs and other visual information.
- **Method:** The pupil is shown shapes on-screen for 3 seconds and asked to identify those shapes from a row of similar shapes on the next screen. The task becomes increasingly difficult as the number of stimulus shapes increases, as does the number of shapes from which the correct options are selected.
- **Score:** The pupil's score feeds into the 'Visual working memory' strand with a weighting of 20 points.
- This probe can be administered online or offline using the downloadable material provided.

Probe 7: Balancing

- **Purpose:** To allow insight into how easily the pupil can automatically balance and manage body position without having to allocate too much conscious attention.
- **Insight provided:** This skill tends to be closely linked to difficulties with gross motor coordination and the ability to multi-task and allocate attention effectively. The pupil who cannot, for example, keep balance while allocating attention to another cognitive task is likely to be the learner who may be able to read aloud fluently but cannot simultaneously absorb the meaning of what is read or who cannot easily make notes while thinking about the content of what is being said or noted.
- **Method:** The pupil is asked to recite some common sequences while first balancing on one leg with eyes open and then with eyes closed.
- **Score:** The pupil's score feeds into the 'Gross motor coordination skills' strand with a weighting of 20 points.
- This probe is administered offline using the downloadable materials provided.

Probe 8: Picture Naming

- **Purpose:** To allow insight into how swiftly the pupil can attach verbal labels to common objects.
- **Insight provided:** Poor naming speed may often be associated with dyslexic difficulties. These are the pupils who need more time to organise and phrase their responses, both spoken and written; who may experience the 'on tip-of-the-tongue' feeling disproportionately often; and who may need extra time in some timed assessments if they are to demonstrate their true level of attainment in the context of timed tests and assessments.
- **Method:** The pupil is asked to look at a series of simple pictures and to name the pictures as fast as possible.
- **Score:** The pupil's score feeds into the 'Processing speed' strand with a weighting of 20 points.
- This probe can be administered online or offline using the downloadable material provided.

4 The Pupil's Voice Record: What's Important to Me?

Why is pupil involvement important?

The answer to this question can be considered under four headings, as follows:

- **Legal:** The legal imperative for promoting children's participation rests on the provisions of the United Nations Convention on the Rights of the Child (UNCRC) which holds the status of international law. Article 12 states that all children have the right to be involved in decisions that affect them. Article 13 grants children the right to express their ideas and information in different ways and is not confined to language alone.

  The English SEND Code of Practice (DfE, 2015)[4] includes a clear expectation that the views and wishes of the pupil will be used to inform decisions about the support he or she needs and that the pupil's views will contribute to an evaluation of the impact of support and intervention. The SEND Code of Practice also requires that schools hold regular discussions relating to pupil progress which should be led by a teacher with good knowledge and understanding of the pupil and who is aware of his or her needs and attainment. This will usually be the class teacher or form tutor, supported by the SENCO. These discussions will need to allow sufficient time to explore the parents'/carers' views and to plan effectively. The views of the pupil should be included in these discussions. This could be through involving the pupil in all or part of the discussion itself or through gathering the pupil's views as part of the preparation.
- **Political:** The political case for participation appears beyond question. Participation engenders positive relationships. It enables children and young people to learn about human rights and democracy. They can be provided with a stake in their environments and communities, thereby reducing conflict. Participation during childhood can be the stepping stone towards adult responsibility.
- **Social:** The social arguments for participation recognise that children and young people are members of every community. Consequently, they have justifiable claims on society, including the right to be regarded and treated with equal worth and status. Promoting participation makes them visible by bringing their needs and views to the attention of adults. Children have needs, feelings and evolving capacities from the day they are born.
- **Practical:** When pupils feel that their views are taken into account, their self-esteem increases, their work improves and they are generally more cooperative with teachers and achieve better results.

---

[4] The Code of Practice is applicable in England. Visit https://www.gov.uk/government/publications/send-code-of-practice-0-to-25

Listening to the pupil's voice

The pupil may have different priorities from those of the adults and it is often important to hear what he or she has to say. **This information is more successfully gathered through interviews and discussions rather than questionnaires, so it does not form part of the SNAP-SpLD reports.** However, it is useful to bear the pupil's priorities in mind as you draw up targets and intervention plans since targets that are important to the pupil are more likely to be achieved.

Before you complete the review with the pupil, you may want to show the parents/carers a copy of the blank record available online, so they know the kinds of information you will be seeking. The pupil also needs to know that his or her parents/carers will be shown the form once it is complete. If it is to be a useful part of the SNAP-SpLD assessment, all relevant people will need to have access to it.

The record can be completed by any adult in school whom the pupil knows and trusts, using a communication style that suits the pupil. This may include using visuals, single words or IT equipment. The pupil is not expected to write as the adult can capture the main points of the pupil's views. Ideally, the adult and the pupil should be in a safe and friendly environment where there is little possibility of interruption.

Although the Pupil's Voice Record: What's Important to Me? can be used by an adult to record the pupil's voice, many schools have their own versions of pupil passports which are just as effective. It is important to recognise that the information recorded is only what the pupil wishes to share; it should not be regarded as a complete picture. Useful areas to include or discuss are listed in Figure 4.1, together with some ideas for prompts which will need to be added to or adapted to meet the age, abilities and context of the individual pupil.

Information to include in the record, and prompts

Figure 4.1 is available as a download in SNAP-SpLD and can be used as the basis for deciding what types of information to include and what questions to ask.

<table>
<tr><td>This is a picture of me ...</td><td>Include a photograph so that any adults who need access to the information know what the pupil looks like.</td></tr>
<tr><td>I want you to know these things about me ...</td><td>Information the pupil wishes to share with adults. This might include, for example:
■ Name and age
□ Particularly the name the pupil likes to be called by
■ Preferred method of communication
□ If the pupil does not speak fluent English, does he or she need an interpreter?
□ If he or she uses Augmentative and Alternative Communication (AAC), which method is he or she most familiar with?
■ Home circumstances
□ Anything the pupil wants to share about his or her family life
■ Diagnoses, disability, medical issues
□ Any formal diagnosis / health issue / hidden disability he or she wishes to share or wants adults to know more about
■ Who is important to the pupil?
□ Any special friends, siblings, family members, teachers, pets</td></tr>
<tr><td>Out of school, I enjoy ...</td><td>■ Explore sports, teams, clubs, lessons, organised groups (e.g. Beavers, Brownies, Scouts, Cadets), religious groups, voluntary work
■ Explore outdoor leisure activities such as roller-skating, fun-parks, skateboarding, BMXing, trampolining, surfboarding, gardening, walking, hiking
■ Explore indoor leisure activities such as playing computer games, playing with friends, social media, art and crafts</td></tr>
<tr><td>In school, I enjoy ...</td><td>■ Explore curriculum areas
■ Explore school clubs and teams
■ Explore social activities and friendships</td></tr>
<tr><td>In school, I want to get better at ...</td><td>Break these down so it's not just 'reading' or 'maths' but more tangible skills that could be broken down into targets. Think about:
■ Specific curriculum skills, for example:
□ Knowing how to write my name
□ Learning multiplication tables
□ Improving handwriting
□ Remembering formulae in maths or science
■ Specific learning skills, for example:
□ Sitting on a carpet spot
□ Remembering to use resources such as pencil grips or reading rulers
□ Remembering to bring books and other equipment to class
□ Listening to instructions
■ Specific social skills, for example:
□ Accepting it if another group wins at playground football
□ Playing with a group of friends
□ Keeping my temper</td></tr>
</table>

<table>
<tr><td>I can help myself by …</td><td>Emphasise that adults can only do so much and that pupils themselves need to take some responsibility for their progress. Base your discussions around strategies which the pupil has not already identified as targets, such as
■ Using equipment, for example:
☐ Putting hearing aids on the recharging station
☐ Using table-top resources such as multiplication squares or spelling lists
☐ Using a timer
☐ Remembering to bring/collect resources
■ Solving problems, for example:
☐ Identifying what the precise problem is
☐ Thinking of different solutions to a problem
☐ Role-playing problem-solving
■ Asking for help, for example:
☐ Telling adults if I don't know what to do
☐ Asking a friend for support
■ Strategies for learning. These will depend on strategies used by the whole class, for example:
☐ Putting up my hand, not shouting out
☐ Listening to instructions
☐ Looking at the teacher, not at a friend
☐ Avoiding distractions
☐ Sitting where I can see the teacher
■ Keeping healthy, for example:
☐ Eating breakfast before school / coming to breakfast club
☐ Bringing a water bottle
☐ Going outside at break times
☐ Remembering to go to the toilet during break</td></tr>
<tr><td>In school, it helps me when …</td><td>This is a specific and realistic list of ideas for things that are useful in the learning environment, for example:
■ The lights are turned off
■ The data projector is turned off when we don't need it
■ I can sit with a friend / by myself / at the front
■ An adult sits next to me / near me
■ I can leave the classroom before the corridors are full of noise and movement
■ People talk in quiet, calm voices
■ I can see pictures / handle objects rather than just hearing people talk
■ I can work outside the classroom</td></tr>
</table>

You can help me by ...	This is a specific and realistic list of ideas for things that teachers can do to help in the classroom, for example: ■ Organisation, for example: □ Talking about my visual timetable (pictorial timetable) at the beginning of each session □ Giving me a visual list of equipment/books needed in the lesson □ Giving a warning 5 minutes before the end of an activity □ Printing out learning objectives / homework to avoid me copying from the board □ Giving additional time to complete activities ■ Accommodations, for example: □ Allowing sensory breaks / time outs □ Allowing me to move around rather than expecting stillness □ Allowing me to use fiddle toys

Figure 4.1: What to include in the Pupil's Voice Record: What's Important to Me?

This is by no means a comprehensive list of ideas to talk about and the items will need to be tailored according to the age of the pupil and what the pupil has already said during your discussions. The outcome should not be an essay but a set of short lists which create a snapshot of a pupil's self-perception of himself or herself as a learner in the context of the classroom or school. The responses can be used to express the pupil's voice in a form like the one shown in Figure 4.1.

5 Administering the SNAP-SpLD questionnaires

Getting started

Your SNAP-SpLD subscription

You can access your SNAP-SpLD subscription from snap.rsassessment.com.

When your subscription expires, you will need to renew it. All of your existing data will continue to be fully available to you, but you will not be able to create any new assessments until your subscription has been renewed.

If you experience any problems in using SNAP-SpLD and the issue is not covered in this User's Handbook, please visit www.rsassessment.com/support to access online guidance for the platform or email onlinesupport@rsassessment.com.

Setting up pupils

Before completing any SNAP-SpLD assessment you will need to add your pupils to the central Admin Hub. If you are already an RS Assessment and MARK customer you may find your pupils have already been set up in Admin Hub, if not, follow the step-by-step guidance in the support hub.

Online requirements

To complete the SNAP-SpLD assessment you will need a tablet/computer with internet access.

Some of the SNAP-SpLD Diagnostic Probes can be administered online. For these you will need a computer or tablet so the pupil can access the test materials. For the probes administered offline/on paper, you will need to enter the scores into the pupil's profile once complete. All of the test materials and score sheets for the probes are available as downloadable PDFs. For those probes which can be completed on-screen, scores will be auto-calculated, but you may want to keep track and score the pupil yourself on paper too.

Paper requirements

Until you are familiar with administering the Diagnostic Probes, you will need to use Chapter 6 in this User's Handbook alongside the probe materials to help you administer and score the tests.

Steps to completing an assessment

When using SNAP-SpLD, the following sequence of steps is likely:

ASSESS

1 Decide whether SNAP-SpLD is an appropriate instrument for the pupil.
2 Select the pupil you want to assess to create a pupil record.

3 Engage the pupil and the pupil's family in the process.
4 Gather data from the family, using the Information from the Family Questionnaire, entering the results online.
5 Use the Pupil Assessment Questionnaire to gather data from the class/ subject teachers, classroom assistants or any other person who is familiar with the pupil's work and behaviour in school.
6 Arrange for the pupil (ideally) to complete the What I Feel Questionnaire, either on a printed copy of the downloadable PDF or answering directly on-screen, and also the Pupil's Voice Record: What's Important to Me? If the pupil answers the questionnaire on paper you will need to enter the results manually online. A copy of the Pupil's Voice Record can be scanned and uploaded to the pupil's profile.
7 Administer the Diagnostic Probes to supplement the results of the Pupil Assessment Questionnaire.

Note: The 'Assess' steps can be carried out in any order and the progress of the assessment can be tracked as each step is completed.

PLAN

8 Generate a Core Profile then the School and Home reports, including the selected interventions.
9 Provide feedback and information to the parents/carers, the pupil and relevant teaching staff and print any relevant Information Sheets.
10 Decide upon a relevant action plan, including possible interventions and timescales.

DO

11 Implement the action plan.

REVIEW

12 Review the pupil's progress at agreed intervals.

This sequence is discussed in more detail below.

ASSESS

Step 1: Is SNAP-SpLD the right instrument for this pupil?

SNAP-SpLD may be used with a pupil who is already well-known to the support services, but it is equally suitable for gaining a comprehensive overview when the first evidence of a learning difficulty is noticed.

Step 2: Create a pupil record

Your SNAP account is accessed from snap.rsassessment.com. Once you have logged in, selecting SNAP Specific Learning Difficulties will take you to the 'Choose' screen. Here you have the option to either assess a new pupil or access a pupil's previous assessment by selecting their name in the list. The 'Show assessment' button will open a pupil's current, or previous assessment, and from here you also have the option to reassess a pupil if you wish.

As noted on page 22, pupils need to be added to the central Admin Hub before a SNAP-SpLD assessment can be completed.

For more information about pupil set up please visit www.rsassessment.com/support to access the online guidance for the platform or email onlinesupport@rsassessment.com.

Step 3: Engage the pupil's family in the process

A sample letter can be downloaded which you can adapt as necessary. Once you have created a SNAP-SpLD profile for the pupil, click on the Letter to Parents/Carers to create a personalised copy as a Word document. Simply save and edit the letter with the pupil's details and amend the 'please return by' date. This letter can then be printed and sent to the parents/carers or, alternatively, the text can be copied and pasted into an email.

Step 4: Complete the Information from the Family Questionnaire

The Information from the Family Questionnaire can be downloaded and printed for the parents/carers to complete. They should be encouraged to answer all the questions they can. Once complete, enter the results online into the pupil's profile.

Step 5: Gather information from school staff for the Pupil Assessment Questionnaire

The Pupil Assessment Questionnaire should be filled in online by a teacher who knows the pupil well. Usually, this will be the pupil's current teacher, but sometimes it may be a previous teacher or a teaching or learning support assistant. At secondary level, learning support / special needs staff are likely to be able to complete most questions, but may wish to draw upon pastoral or subject staff as appropriate. Where classroom staff have not been able to answer a question, the SENCO should do so if possible.

An ideal scenario might be for school staff who know the pupil to answer the questions together, sharing their views and thereby making the answers less subjective, but often this will not be practical. Where there are conflicting answers to a question, the answer entered will depend upon the SENCO's professional judgement.

The questionnaire presents a series of questions relating to the pupil's learning characteristics.

Step 6: Complete the What I Feel Questionnaire and the Pupil's Voice Record: What's Important to Me? (both optional)

If you wish to include self-esteem as part of the SNAP-SpLD analysis, arrange for the pupil to complete the What I Feel Questionnaire online or on the printed downloadable PDF, with or without adult assistance, or arrange for a suitable adult to complete it. Clearly, self-esteem is best accessed by self-report and the questions are phrased for direct response by the pupil. However, where it is considered that a learner is not sufficiently mature to fill in the questionnaire, the questions may be completed by an adult who knows the pupil well. This can be done in collaboration with the pupil, or not, whichever is deemed best for that individual.

While completing the What I Feel Questionnaire, you should take the opportunity to capture the pupil's voice using the Pupil's Voice Record: What's Important to Me? The record should be completed with somebody who knows the pupil well and whom the pupil trusts. It is not expected that the pupil should complete the record themselves, rather that the adult will scribe for them. Use the prompts in Chapter 4 to probe what really matters to the pupil and how he or she feels about his or her learning. Once complete, a scanned copy of the Pupil's Voice Record can be uploaded and saved to the pupil's profile.

Note: The academic self-esteem and social self-esteem sections in the Core Profile will only generate if the What I Feel Questionnaire is completed.

Step 7: Administer the Diagnostic Probes

In the Diagnostic Probes section online you will find a list of all the probes. For each one you can download the score sheet and any supporting materials. Instructions for administering each probe can be found in Chapter 6.

Some of the Diagnostic Probes need to be administered on-screen and scores will be auto-calculated, but for all of them it's recommended the score sheet is downloaded, printed and completed for you to keep track and score as the pupil carries out the tasks. For those probes administered offline, scores will need to be entered and recorded in the pupil's profile once complete.

On the individual score sheets:

- Enter the pupil's score for each item, using **1** for correct answers and **0** for incorrect answers.
- For **Probe 4: Timed Text Copying**, enter:
  - the number of words copied in 1 minute
  - the number of marks that need to be deducted for each incorrect word/punctuation
  - the number of marks that need to be deducted for untidy handwriting (1 = slightly untidy, 2 = very untidy, 3 = difficult to read).
- For **Probe 7: Balancing**, enter the score that best describes the pupil's balance, both with eyes open and eyes closed.
- For **Probe 8: Picture Naming**, enter the number of seconds taken for both item 1 and 2.
- Enter the total scores online, the system will then translate these and the data will feed into the pupil's Core Profile.

PLAN

Step 8: Profile the pupil's strengths and difficulties

Once the questionnaires have been completed, you can generate a Core Profile which is a bar chart showing the apparent prominence of each of the main strands, either as specific strengths or difficulties. The Core Profile can be downloaded and printed if required. In the downloadable version of the Core Profile the pupil's principal strengths and weaknesses will be listed with a brief description.

You do not need to answer all of the questions or do all of the probes for a profile to be generated. It is perfectly valid, for example, just to complete the Pupil Assessment Questionnaire, and omit some or all of the probes. But obviously, the more information, the better and more valid the resulting profile. Ideally the Pupil Assessment Questionnaire and Information from the Family Questionnaire should be completed in full, and all of the probes. (The self-esteem section of the Core Profile will be completed only if the What I Feel Questionnaire is done by the pupil, or with support.)

Which SpLDs should be seen as significant?

Checklists for specific learning difficulties include characteristics that will be seen in many pupils who have no difficulties with their learning. For example, a pupil can be inattentive, may have been an unusually demanding infant or may have unusual posture when reading, without any of these being in themselves an indicator of a SpLD.

A SpLD is seen to be present only when a significant cluster of characteristics is present. All of us show some signs, but far fewer of us show enough signs to suggest a specific difficulty. By definition, then, answering all of the SNAP-SpLD questions about SpLD characteristics will produce some indicators for any pupil. It is only when some notional critical threshold is passed that the cluster of characteristics become potentially significant. In deciding which SpLDs are significant, it is not helpful to suggest precise guidelines and cut-off points. But it seems a helpful rule of thumb to assume that **no more than two or three should be addressed at one time**. Exactly which they should be remains a matter for individual judgement in each case, but note that separate School and Home reports need to be generated for each area you would like to address.

Patterns of SpLDs and conditions that might be expected

The purpose of SNAP-SpLD is to penetrate beyond the existing 'shorthand' labels and the combinations of difficulties they imply – every individual's SpLD is likely to be made up of a unique combination of strands. Some combinations might be expected more often than others and some combinations may be diagnostically very revealing.

For example, it is to be expected that literacy difficulties will be accompanied by one or more of the working memory difficulties, processing speed difficulties, some visual processing difficulties or phonological difficulties. Such an array would constitute a 'classic dyslexic' profile.

Conversely, literacy difficulties accompanied only by attention difficulties or hyperactivity might suggest that the literacy difficulty is not a co-morbid difficulty as such (i.e. a coinciding intrinsic difficulty). It seems more probable that attentional and hyperactivity difficulties have stood in the way of the pupil's acquisition of literacy, rather than literacy being delayed for intrinsic reasons.

Because ADHD and dyslexia are often genuinely co-morbid, such a pattern might also raise further questions already alluded to above: is it more probable that this pupil's high score for attentional and hyperactive factors is due to social, emotional or environmental factors rather than the intrinsic neurological or physiological factors implied by a formal diagnosis of ADD or ADHD? You will need to depend upon your own professional judgement for fine distinctions such as these; and if SNAP-SpLD is being used to guide decisions about onward referral, then the SNAP profile should add a valuable extra dimension to the outcomes of the referral.

Step 9: Provide feedback and information to parents/carers, teaching staff/support staff and the pupil

Sharing information with all parties concerned is critical. Discussion with the pupil should arise naturally out of the pupil's voice process. The Core Profile should be used during a meeting with the parents/carers to discuss the relative strengths and needs of the pupil. All relevant teaching staff should also share in this information. For more detailed information about each of the most prominent conditions, an Information Sheet can be accessed (in the SNAP-SpLD Resources Bank) and printed out for both teachers and parents/carers to share key information about the difficulties that seem most significant.

Step 10: Decide on a plan of action

Tips and advice

A number of general strategies, tips and advice, plus online and printed sources of information, are provided in both the School Report and the Home Report, tailored specifically for teachers/support staff and parents/carers respectively. Both teaching staff and parents/carers should be encouraged to implement the activities and advice suggested for managing the particular learning difficulty identified either at school or at home. Sharing these reports and using them as the basis for action planning is a critical component in the *Assess, Plan, Do, Review* model.

SpLDs seldom exist in isolation, so it is likely that there will be more than one prominent difficulty on a pupil's Core Profile. The downloadable and printable version of the Core Profile will list the top three most significant strengths and difficulties, but you should use your professional judgement about which and how many to act upon and this can be done via the 'Plan, Do and Review' section online, when generating the School and Home reports. Separate School and Home reports will need to be generated for each area SNAP-SpLD profiles. Together, the school, pupil and parent/carer need to devise realistic and measurable targets to address the difficulty. The school, in particular, should focus on how to show progress and impact.

Interventions

As described above, users will need to interpret each Core Profile in the context of their own experiences, circumstances and resources. However, to assist with planning relevant interventions to suit the pupil, SNAP-SpLD generates a list of intervention resources specific to the child's age and areas of difficulty from which you can select the most relevant.

Once selected, these interventions are then inserted into both the School Report (providing either guidance to implement the intervention or a web address to go to for more information), as well as the Home Report (providing an overview of what interventions the school plans to implement), when these reports are generated.

The advice provided in these reports should be regarded as a pick 'n' mix resource bank of ideas that can be combined with the ideas, resources and approaches already in use in the school, according to the combination of difficulties experienced by each pupil. The School and Home reports are both generated as Word documents, so it is possible to edit them in whichever way you think it appropriate. Not all of the advice will be suited to every pupil with that difficulty, so you should select according to your knowledge of the pupil and also use ideas from other sections if they would suit the pupil. Where particular resources are referred to, they should be seen as examples only, as there will be many other resources of equal value since new resources are being developed and published continuously.

DO

Step 11: Implementation of the action plan

There is now a period of implementation, whilst the intervention is carried out. During this time, the SENCO/teachers involved should carefully monitor the progress of the pupil, making notes about any strategies and resources which have been particularly helpful and any improvements that have been made.

REVIEW

Step 12: Review progress

At the agreed date, the progress of the pupil should be reviewed and discussed with both the pupil and the parents/carers. It is possible to create multiple assessments for each pupil and SNAP-SpLD allows you to select up to three previous Core Profiles to compare. Re-assessment means that you can explore whether an intervention should be continued, expanded on, replaced with something different or stopped. This review process enables progress to be celebrated and allows all concerned to feel actively involved and responsible for making any necessary changes to ensure a positive outcome. In addition, if a referral is made to other agencies, the school has a record of everything that has been undertaken together with focused data on the effects of the intervention programme implemented. Such information could be of considerable value as a starting point.

6 Administering the Diagnostic Probes
Probe 1A
Reading for Understanding

In this test, the pupil reads a passage on the screen, reads the questions and then selects the correct answers from a choice of four responses.

Equipment required

- Tablet/computer for displaying the test materials to the pupil (and for entering the final score if the probe is administered offline, on paper).
- Downloaded and printed passages, questions and score sheet if you prefer to administer this probe offline.

Instructions for the test administrator

- Seat the pupil with the tablet/computer.
- Read aloud the instructions below, explaining anything as needed.
- Work through the practice item with the pupil. You can read the practice item aloud if you think it may be a little hard.
- Start the test. It will auto-score as the pupil works through the questions on-screen, but you can keep track of the scores if you wish on the printed score sheet. **Score 1 if correct, 0 if incorrect**.
- There is no **'discontinue'** rule so allow the pupil to go as far as he or she feels they can. But you can discontinue if it seems that the pupil is getting upset or is obviously trying items that are too hard. Just say: *'Well done and that's as far as we go with these'*. Exit the test on-screen, the pupil's final score will be recorded.

Instructions to be read out to the pupil

- *You are going to see some sentences and short passages. Read each one when it appears on the screen. Read the question, and then choose the right answer.*
- *Take as long as you like over each one. There is no time limit.*
- *Just move on to the next screen when you have answered the question.*
- *The questions get harder and harder. Go as far as you can and just stop when they get too difficult.*
- *We'll have a look at an example before you start.*

Complete the practice question.

- *Now let's try some other ones.*

Complete the test questions.

Probe 1B
Listening for Understanding

In this test, the pupil listens to any passage/s that were not achieved in Probe 1A: Reading for Understanding. The pupil then listens to (and sees on-screen) the questions and answer options again, before selecting the correct answer from the choice of four responses.

Equipment required

- Tablet/computer for displaying the test materials to the pupil and for entering the final score (only if the probe is administered offline)
- Downloaded and printed score sheet for recording scores, including the results from Probe 1A: Reading for Understanding to determine which items to use as listening questions
- Script for the test administrator with the passages and questions to read out to the pupil

Instructions for the test administrator

- This probe must come **after** Probe 1A: Reading for Understanding.
- **Only items which were not achieved in Probe 1A: Reading for Understanding (including both incorrect items and those which were not attempted will be presented to the pupil on-screen).**
- Seat the pupil with the tablet/computer.
- Read aloud the instructions below, explaining anything as needed.
- Work through the practice item with the pupil, using the 'Script for the test administrator' on page 32.

In this test, the pupil only does the items he or she couldn't manage in Probe 1A. Therefore, start with the ones the pupil got wrong, then move on to the ones he or she didn't try when reading them. If administering this probe online, only the passages and questions the pupil got wrong will be displayed. For a Probe 1 score sheet like Figure 6.1 on the next page:

Start with item 4.

- You don't need to do item 5 – that was got right when reading it, and treat it as a correct response in this test too – give it a mark on the Probe 1b score sheet as if it had been done right as a listening task.

Then do items 6 and 7.

- You don't need to do item 8 – that was got right when reading it, and treat it as a correct response in this test too – give it a mark as if it had been done right as a listening task.
- Then do item 9 and go on until the pupil gives three consecutive wrong answers.

Question	Correct response	Pupil score (1/0)
Practise item	b	n/a
1	a	1
2	b	1
3	d	1
4	b	0
5	c	1
6	a	0
7	d	0
8	c	1
9	a	0
10	a	0
11	c	not attempted
12	b	not attempted
13	b	not attempted
14	a	not attempted
15	b	not attempted
		Total score:

Figure 6.1: Example Probe 1 score sheet

- Start the test. Read each passage, question and the four responses **twice** (making sure the pupil can't see them on your passage sheet), while the learner is looking at the options on his or her screen.
- Give the pupil as long as needed to study the options and choose the answer.
- If administering the probe offline, record the scores. **Score 1 if correct, 0 if incorrect.** If administering the probe on-screen it will score automatically.
- **Discontinue after 3 consecutive incorrect responses.** You can discontinue before that if it seems that the pupil is getting upset or is obviously trying items that are too hard. Just say: *'Well done and that's as far as we go with these'.* Exit the test on-screen, the pupil's final score will be recorded.

Instructions to be read out to the pupil

- *Here are some of the same sentences and questions you have just worked on, but this time they will be read to you instead of reading them yourself as you did last time.*
- *You will hear each passage and question and the four choices twice. After the second hearing, you make your choice.*
- *Take as long as you like over each one. There is no time limit.*
- *You will see the questions and choices on the screen to help you remember them, but you won't see the passages – you will only hear them.*
- *Let's start with a practice one.*

Complete the practice question.

- *Now let's try some other ones.*

Complete the test questions.

Script for the test administrator

Practice question

Even though he wasn't hungry, the new puppy chewed everything when he was left alone in the house, so mum made sure there was someone with him as much as possible.

When did the puppy chew things?

a. When mum was with him.

b. When no-one was with him.

c. When there was someone with him as much as possible.

d. When he was hungry.

Question 1

Ali was in his room with Sam.

Where was Ali?

a. In his room

b. In Sam's room

c. On his own in his room

d. On his own in Sam's room

Question 2

It was too hot in the garden. The boys went indoors.

Why did the boys go indoors?

a. It was hot indoors.

b. The garden was very hot.

c. It was cold in the garden.

d. It was cold in the garden and indoors.

Question 3

It was a very cold winter day, and Sara was glad that she and her sister Jen had hats and gloves.

Why did Sara have a hat on?

a. Because she had her gloves on.

b. Because Jen had her hat on.

c. Because she was with her sister.

d. Because it was a cold day in the winter.

Question 4

The boys were sad. They had to miss the end of term party at school.

Why were they sad?

a. It was the end of term.

b. They could not go to the party.

c. There was a party at school.

d. They did not enjoy the party.

Question 5

It was a very fast train, but there was thick fog, and it was ten minutes late at the station.

Why was the train late?

a. It was not a very fast train.

b. It stayed at the station ten minutes too long.

c. The weather meant it had to go more slowly.

d. For ten minutes there was thick fog at the station.

Question 6

There were lots of families in the shopping centre. All the children were very excited as the holidays were only three weeks away. It was a wet and rainy afternoon, so families were getting their shopping done rather than doing things outdoors.

Why were the shops very busy?

a. Because of the bad weather.

b. Because the children were very excited.

c. Because the holidays were three weeks ago.

d. Because the holidays were only three weeks away.

Question 7

The wind made a strange, sad sound in the trees. The girls were scared and hurried through the wood. They just wanted to be at home.

Why were the girls scared?

a. Because they felt sad and strange.

b. Because they wanted to get home.

c. Because they hurried through the wood.

d. Because the sound of the wind scared them.

Question 8

The weather was quickly deteriorating. The three climbers noticed that the mountain top could no longer be seen – a thin rain hid it from view, and the wind was getting stronger. They decided to turn back before it was too late.

What does 'deteriorating' mean?

1. Getting misty
2. Getting colder
3. Getting worse
4. Quickly changing

Question 9

History often suggests that the Vikings were sea-going raiders and fighters, roaming the seas in their long ships, looting and plundering and terrifying people wherever they came ashore. However, most of those who sailed to new lands were primarily traders and farmers seeking new markets for trade and new places to settle with their families.

What was usually the reason for Vikings to sail overseas?

a. They were looking for new people to trade with and new places to live.

b. That is what Vikings always did – sailing overseas in their long ships, fighting and raiding.

c. They were looking for traders and farmers to raid, loot and plunder.

d. To terrify people wherever they came ashore.

Question 10

People love to meet up with old friends. It provides a chance to catch up on each other's news, as well as helping sustain the friendship. Often our friends may be the people who matter most to us, influencing us perhaps more than our families do as we grow older. Perhaps this is because we choose our friends but we can't choose our families in the same way.

Why are friends so important to us?

a. They influence us, often more than our families do.

b. They allow us to catch up on each other's news.

c. It is lovely to meet up with them.

d. They help us sustain our relationship.

Question 11

In some societies and cultures in the past, the gods were appeased by sacrifices. It was believed that this would cause them to smile upon the people and bring them good harvests and success in war.

What does the phrase 'smile upon the people' mean?

a. Help them with the sacrifices

b. Sacrifices people

c. Made to feel happy and helpful towards the people

d. Cause wars and harvests

Question 12

Computers have changed and enhanced our lives in countless ways over recent years. Not least, our access to unlimited complex information is instantaneous. A few clicks will bring to your screen information, archives and records that, thirty years ago, could be accessed only by visiting libraries, museums, newspaper archives, record offices and countless other specialist sources. Now all this information comes to you on your screen, wherever you might be.

What is the meaning of the word 'enhanced' in this passage?

a. Changed our lives

b. Improved our lives

c. Allowed access to complex information wherever we are

d. Saved us from having to visit libraries, archives and record offices

Question 13

Instinctively we tense ourselves when we sense we are being threatened in any way – when, for example, we perceive a sudden physical movement as a precursor to an assault of some kind; or when perhaps we hear a sound that has in the past been the prelude to a seriously unpleasant experience. Flinching in this way is an instinctive and automatic reaction, and one that can be very hard to control.

From the passage, which of these statements is true?

a. Flinching is a prelude to being assaulted.

b. Flinching is an involuntary physical movement.

c. Flinching is a seriously unpleasant experience.

d. Flinching is caused by hearing a sound that we have heard before.

Question 14

'Parenting style' is a way of thinking about the standard strategies that parents use in their child-rearing. They are the representations of how parents respond to the demands of their children. Children go through different stages in life, and parents create their own parenting styles from a combination of factors that evolve over time as children begin to develop their own personalities. During the stage of infancy, parents try to adjust to a new lifestyle in terms of adapting and bonding with their new infant. In the stage of adolescence, parents encounter new challenges such as adolescents seeking and desiring freedom. A child's temperament and the parents' cultural patterns have an influence on the kind of parenting style a child may receive.

Which of these statements best reflects the gist of the whole passage?

a. How parents react to their children depends on their own cultural backgrounds and the developing age and needs of the child.

b. Children's personalities change and develop as they grow older.

c. Parenting an infant means adjusting to a completely new lifestyle as the parents learn to adapt and bond with the new infant.

d. Adolescents may be particularly challenging for parents, as the young person seeks and desires freedom in a way that a younger child does not.

Question 15

Moral relativism is the view that moral judgements are true or false only relative to some particular standpoint (for instance, that of a culture or a historical period) and that no standpoint is uniquely privileged over all others. Moral relativism has been increasingly accepted as the primary moral philosophy of modern Western society, a culture that was previously governed by a 'Judeo-Christian' view of morality. While these Judeo-Christian standards continue to be the foundation for civil law, many people hold to the concept that right or wrong are not absolutes, but can and should be determined by each individual. In increasingly pluralistic societies, too, where Judeo-Christian ethics may be increasingly challenged, or enriched, by ethics derived from other religions and belief, moral relativism in some form may become increasingly central to how many of us think.

Which of these statements best reflects the gist of the whole passage?

a. Moral relativism is uniquely privileged over all other moral standpoints.

b. The changing nature of society brings with it changing ethics and values that may often challenge the moral basis for our values.

c. Moral relativism provides the foundations for Judeo-Christian ethics.

d. Judeo-Christian beliefs hold that no one standpoint is uniquely privileged over others.

Probe 2A

Phonological Awareness: Sound Deletion

In this test, non-words are read to the pupil. The pupil has to repeat them back, but with a sound omitted.

Equipment required

- Printed and downloaded score sheet for recording scores
- Tablet/computer for recording the final score

Instructions for the test administrator

- Read aloud the instructions below, explaining anything as needed.
- Work through the practice items with the pupil, using the 'Script for the test administrator' on the next page. If necessary, discuss the examples with the pupil until they get them correct.
- If he or she is really struggling to understand the concept, it is sometimes useful to write down the example non-words on a piece of paper. Get the pupil to cover up with their finger the sound they are taking out, then to sound out what is left.
- Do not, however, write down the non-words when doing the test questions. The pupil must be able to 'delete' the sound from only hearing the non-word, without seeing it written down.
- Start the test, recording the scores. **Score 1 if correct, 0 if incorrect**. Once complete, enter the pupil's score in their profile.
- **Discontinue after 3 consecutive incorrect responses** or if the task is clearly too hard for the pupil. Just say: '*Well done and that's as far as we go with these.*'

Instructions to be read out to the pupil

- *In this task, you have to take a sound out of a word and work out what the new word is that you are left with.*
- *We are going to use made-up words, so you will not have heard them before.*
- *Let's try two as practice so that you can see what I mean. You will need to listen very carefully.*

Read the practice items.

- *Now let's try some other ones.*

Read the test items.

Script for the test administrator

	Item to be read out to the pupil
Practice 1	*rusp, rusp* *What do you get if you take the /r/ out of rusp?*
Practice 2	*glup, glup* *What do you get if you take the /l/ out of glup?*
1	*gloof, gloof* *Take the /g/ out of gloof.*
2	*shumper, shumper* *Take the /sh/ out of shumper.*
3	*chid, chid* *Take the /ch/ out of chid.*
4	*yopa, yopa* *Take the /y/ out of yopa.*
5	*bubintin, bubintin* *Take the /tin/ out of bubintin.*
6	*spug, spug* *Take the /p/ out of spug.*
7	*framp, framp* *Take the /r/ out of framp.*
8	*slooch, slooch* *Take the /l/ out of slooch.*
9	*rumdell, rumdell* *Take the /d/ out of rumdell.*
10	*jegmoff, jegmoff* *Take the /m/ out of jegmoff.*

Probe 2B

Phonological Awareness: Non-word Decoding

In this test, the pupil reads non-words aloud. Each screen shows some non-words; the pupil navigates through the screens, reading them aloud.

Equipment required

- Tablet/computer for displaying the test materials to the pupil and entering the final score
- Downloaded and printed guidance and score sheet for recording scores
- The test materials are also available to download if you would prefer to administer this probe offline

Instructions for the test administrator

- Seat the pupil at the tablet/computer.
- Read aloud the instructions below, explaining anything as needed.
- Work through the practice items with the pupil. If necessary, discuss and demonstrate the examples until he or she gets them correct.
- Start the test, using the guidance provided on the downloadable score sheet for acceptable pronunciations and recording the scores. **Score 1 if correct, 0 if incorrect**. Once complete, enter the pupil's score in their profile.
- Discontinue after 6 consecutive incorrect responses or if the pupil is clearly finding it too hard. Just say: '*Well done and that's as far as we go with these.*'

Instructions to be read out to the pupil

- *It can be useful to see how people read made-up words.*
- *We're going to practise on the first three, then you can try the rest on your own.*
- *You will never have seen them before, because they are made-up words!*
- *Ready? So, read aloud the practice words on the screen.*

Complete the practice words.

- *Now let's try some other ones. Just read as many as you can, scrolling on to the next screen as soon as you are ready.*

Complete the test words.

Probe 3
Spelling

In this test, the pupil spells a sequence of increasingly difficult words.

Equipment required

- Script for the test administrator with the words to be spelled and their context sentences
- Downloaded and printed score sheet for recording scores
- Tablet/computer for entering the final score
- Lined paper, pencil and eraser

Instructions for the test administrator

- Read aloud the instructions below, explaining anything as needed.
- Work through the practice items with the pupil, using the 'Script for the test administrator' on the next page.
- Start the test, recording the responses. **Score 1 if correct, 0 if incorrect**. Once complete, enter the pupil's score in their profile.
- Discontinue after 4 consecutive incorrect responses or earlier than that if you judge that the pupil is becoming distressed or evidently unable to cope. Just say: '*Well done and that's as far as we go with these.*'

Instructions to be read out to the pupil

- *We're going to look at how easily you can spell words.*
- *They will be quite easy to begin with, but they get more difficult as you go on.*
- *I will say the word, then say it again in a sentence, and then say it once again before you write it down on your sheet.*
- *You just need to write down the word, not the whole sentence.*
- *Let's do two as practice first.*

Read the practice items.

- *Now let's try some other ones.*

Read the test items.

Script for the test administrator

	Items to be read out to the pupil
Practice 1	*cat – The cat lay in the sun. – cat*
Practice 2	*went – We went to London. – went*
	Items to be read out to the pupil
1	*mat – A mat is like a little carpet. – mat*
2	*dog – He gave the dog a bone. – dog*
3	*bed – She bought a new bed. – bed*
4	*tree – The leaves fell off the tree. – tree*
5	*lift – They took the lift up to the top floor. – lift*
6	*list – He made a list of toys he wanted. – list*
7	*boat – They sailed the boat across the bay. – boat*
8	*song – The song was fun to sing. – song*
9	*twelve – There are twelve months in the year. – twelve*
10	*swimming – She went to swimming lessons after school. – swimming*
11	*perfect – The weather was perfect. – perfect*
12	*world – He sailed around the world. – world*
13	*elephant – The children saw the elephant at the zoo. – elephant*
14	*scissors – Sam cut out the shape with some scissors. – scissors*
15	*reason – David had no reason to hit his brother. – reason*
16	*frightened – The little girl was frightened of the dark. – frightened*
17	*innocent – The prisoner said that he was innocent. – innocent*
18	*anxious – She was late home and her father was getting anxious. – anxious*
19	*refrigeration – Refrigeration is just one way of preserving food. – refrigeration*
20	*superfluous – She was obviously not needed, and felt superfluous from the start. – superfluous*

Probe 4
Timed Text Copying

In this test, the pupil copies text at his or her normal writing speed.

Equipment required

- Downloaded Text Copying Sheet for the pupil, Passage 1 (7–8 years) or Passage 2 (9–16 years)
- Pen/pencil
- Stopwatch/timer
- Downloaded and printed score sheet for recording scores
- Tablet/computer for entering the final score

Instructions for the test administrator

- Give the pupil the appropriate Text Copying Sheet:
  - □ Passage 1 for pupils aged 7–8 years
  - □ Passage 2 for pupils aged 9–16 years
- Read aloud the instructions below, explaining anything as needed.
- When the pupil is ready, start the test and the stopwatch/timer. Stop the pupil after exactly **1 minute**.
- Score by counting the number of words copied in 1 minute.
- Deduct a mark for each incorrect word/punctuation.
- Deduct the following marks for handwriting:
  - □ deduct 1 mark for slightly untidy writing
  - □ deduct 2 marks for very untidy writing
  - □ deduct 3 marks for writing that is difficult to read.
- Once complete, enter the pupil's score in their profile.

Instructions to be read out to the pupil

- *We're going to look at how you copy some sentences.*
- *Here they are on a sheet, and I'll read them out to you. Then you copy them underneath.*
- *Write at your normal writing speed – don't hurry, but don't go really carefully either. Just go at your normal speed.*
- *Start when I tell you and I'll stop you after 1 minute.*
- *Are you ready? Start now.*

Start the timer.

Probe 5
Backward Span

In this test, the pupil listens to increasingly long lists of words and repeats them in reverse order.

Equipment required

- Downloaded and printed test words and score sheet for recording scores
- Tablet/computer for entering the final score

Instructions for the test administrator

- Read aloud the instructions below, explaining anything as needed.
- Start the test, using the 'Script for the test administrator' on the next page.
- Record the scores. Score each item as:
  - 1 = all correct and in correct order
  - 0 = incorrect in any way
- Discontinue after 3 consecutive scores of 0. Once complete, enter the pupil's score in their profile.

Instructions to be read out to the pupil

- *I'm going to say some words. Then I want you to say them backwards.*
- *I'll show you what I mean.*
- *If I say 'bus, book', you say 'book, bus'.*
- *Or, if I say 'apple, piano, football', you say 'football, piano, apple'.*
- *Now you try. I'll say some words, and then you say them backwards.*
- *To begin with, there are only two words to remember and repeat backwards. As we go on there will be more words.*

Script for the test administrator

	Items to be read out to the pupil						
1	*cat*	*frog*					
2	*lorry*	*coat*					
3	*fork*	*zebra*					
4	*mug*	*snake*	*chair*				
5	*book*	*knife*	*house*				
6	*door*	*ferry*	*car*				
7	*jet*	*horse*	*dress*	*shoe*			
8	*coal*	*girl*	*goat*	*butterfly*			
9	*bike*	*skis*	*purse*	*bowl*			
10	*shoe*	*cow*	*tree*	*van*	*table*		
11	*pan*	*flower*	*taxi*	*bus*	*road*		
12	*spoon*	*orange*	*tie*	*toast*	*boat*		
13	*cooker*	*shirt*	*gerbil*	*wall*	*sausage*	*plane*	
14	*car*	*chair*	*giraffe*	*gate*	*pot*	*shed*	
15	*bird*	*shoe*	*trousers*	*grass*	*clock*	*skates*	
16	*rug*	*plate*	*glasses*	*pig*	*sugar*	*sock*	*cream*
17	*mouse*	*cup*	*egg*	*hat*	*dog*	*glove*	*bicycle*
18	*dish*	*towel*	*scarf*	*rabbit*	*carpet*	*watch*	*scooter*

Probe 6
Visual Memory

This test probes visual memory by displaying an abstract shape/s for 3 seconds on-screen, then asking the pupil to identify them from an array of shapes.

Equipment required

- Tablet/computer for displaying the test to the pupil and/or entering the final score
- Downloaded and printed marker's guide and score sheet for recording scores
- Downloaded test material if you would prefer to administer the probe offline

Instructions for the test administrator

- Seat the pupil with the tablet/computer.
- Read aloud the instructions below, explaining anything as needed.
- Work through the practice items with the pupil.
- Start the test.
- The test will auto-score if administered on-screen. If administered offline record the scores, **score 1 if correct, 0 if incorrect**.
- **Discontinue after 3 consecutive incorrect responses** or when the pupil is evidently struggling. Just say: *'Well done and that's as far as we go with these'*. Exit the test on-screen, the pupil's final score will be recorded.

Instructions to be read out to the pupil

- *In this task, you look at one or more shapes on the screen for 3 seconds.*
- *After 3 seconds, the screen will move on and you can choose which shape or shapes matches the one or ones you have just seen.*
- *We'll do two examples together and then you can try some on your own.*

Complete the practice items.

- *Now let's try some other ones.*

Complete the test items.

Probe 7
Balancing Sequencing Tasks

This test involves observing and noting a pupil's ability to balance while his or her attention is focused on another task. The testing involves:

1 Establishing which leg the pupil favours for balancing.
2 Identifying the two sequencing tasks to be used.
3 Carrying out the balancing tasks.

Equipment required

- A sturdy book or books to stand on, longer than the pupil's foot and between 4 cm and 10 cm high
- A ball big enough to kick (optional)
- Downloaded and printed score sheet for recording scores
- Tablet/computer for entering the final score

Instructions to the test administrator

Important: For safety reasons, carry out this task in an open space away from any furniture or sharp edges, etc. which may cause the pupil injury if he or she were to overbalance. The book/s must not be more than 10cm high.

1 Establish **which leg the pupil favours for balancing** (if unsure which is their dominant foot, get them to kick a ball to see):
   - If right-footed, ask the pupil to balance on the left leg.
   - If left-footed, ask the pupil to balance on the right leg.

2 Identify the sequencing task to be used: Work through the reciting and counting tasks (Sections 1 and 2 in the 'Instructions to be read out to the pupil' on the next page) with the pupil seated and eyes open. Identify **one task from each section** that he or she seems to have to think about, that is he or she can do with at least some success but only by thinking about it and not doing it automatically and without conscious thought. When you have found out which reciting task and counting backwards task are best for the pupil, read the instructions out to them.

3 Carry out the balancing task:
   - Ask the pupil to do the chosen reciting task, while balancing on the book, on one leg, with eyes open.
   - Use the guidance provided on the score sheet to determine a score from 0–6.
   - Then ask the pupil to do the chosen counting task while balancing on the book, on one leg, with eyes closed.

- Use the guidance provided on the score sheet to determine a score from 0–6.
- Add the two scores to produce a total score out of 12 (where 12 means excellent balance and 0 means very poor balance).

Important: Your focus is solely upon the pupil's ability to *balance* – the accuracy of the answers does not matter at all. If the pupil is finding the task too easy after all, and is not having to think about it, repeat the process with a more demanding task and use this to derive the total score.

Instructions to be read out to the pupil

- *We are now going to explore how easy it is for you to keep your balance on one leg while you are thinking about something else.*
- *First we are going to find some tasks that make you think a bit …*

Section 1 Reciting tasks

- *Can you …*
  - ☐ *Recite the days of the week?*
  - ☐ *Recite the days of the week backwards?*
  - ☐ *Recite the months of the year?*
  - ☐ *Recite the months of the year backwards?*
  - ☐ *Recite the months of the year backwards, leaving out any month starting with the letter J?*
  - ☐ *Recite the months of the year backwards, leaving out any month starting with the letter J or A?*

Section 2 Counting backwards

- *Can you …*
  - ☐ *Count backwards from 10?*
  - ☐ *Count backwards from 20?*
  - ☐ *Count backwards from 20 in steps of 2?*
  - ☐ *Count backwards from 20 in steps of 3?*
  - ☐ *Count backwards from 50, leaving out any number that includes the digit 7?*
  - ☐ *Count backwards from 50, leaving out any number that includes the digit 7 or the digit 3?*
- *Now you are going to do the reciting task* [state task chosen] *while standing on the book on one leg, with your eyes open. Try as hard as you can to stay balanced.*

Complete task.

- *Now you are going to do the counting task* [state task chosen] *while standing on the book on one leg, with your eyes closed. Try as hard as you can to stay balanced.*

Complete task.

Probe 8
Picture Naming

In this test, the pupil names all the items on the screen sequentially and the time taken to do so is recorded.

Equipment required

- Tablet/computer for displaying the test to the pupil and entering the final score
- Stopwatch/timer (if administering offline)
- Downloaded and printed score sheet for recording scores
- Downloaded and printed test materials if you would prefer to administer the probe offline

Instructions for the test administrator

- Seat the pupil at the tablet/computer.
- Read aloud the instructions below, explaining anything as needed.
- If administering the probe offline, start the timer when the pupil is ready and stop when he or she has finished that item.

  Record the times taken. If administering the probe online, there is a timer which will start after the child has completed the practice question. The timer begins for each item when you click 'start' and is stopped when you click 'finish'. The final total time appears in the child's profile once the test is complete.
- Do not penalise or correct any stumbling, pauses or incorrect calls – you are interested only in the lapse of time between start and finish.

Instructions to be read out to the pupil

- *I'm going to ask you to look at some pictures on the screen, and then name them as fast as you can.*
- *We'll practise first with the pictures on the first screen.*
- *They show a butterfly, a cat, a fish, a rabbit and a horse. Now you name them as fast as you can.*

Show practice item. Note that the pupil does not have to say the determiner 'a' or 'the'.

- *Now let's do two more. Try this one first. Name them as fast as you can.*

Show Item 1.

- *Are you ready? Start now.*

Start the timer.

- *Now let's do the second one. Remember to go as fast as you can.*

Show Item 2.

- *Are you ready? Start now.*

Start the timer.

7 The development and rationale of SNAP-SpLD

Background to this version

SNAP-SpLD 4–16 builds on and extends the previous versions of SNAP Infant Check 4–6 years and SNAP-SpLD 7–16 years. It is an instrument that has been under a process of continuous review and development since Version 1, through Versions 2 and 3, and has now resulted in this combined online version, SNAP-SpLD 4–16. For each new version, the information sheets and reports have been updated and the skill strands reviewed and reorganised. The underlying matrix of scores and weightings remained unchanged through Versions 1–3; however, it has it has been entirely rebuilt for this online version of SNAP-SpLD 4–16.

The rebuilding has been based on a process of iteration and refinement, passing back and forth between the SNAP matrix and a parallel matrix used in the school-based and independent educational psychology assessments of one of the authors. The evident value of the original SNAP matrix suggested a valuable role for it in educational psychology assessments, and a version was accordingly developed for this purpose. This continuously evolving version remained in continuous use of a period of ten years or so, informing assessments in both school settings and independent assessments.

This context allowed for a process of constant feedback and adjustment – strands were included or dropped, weightings adjusted and questions adapted to reflect the continuous feedback from pupils, teaching staff and families and from the educational psychology assessments that typically followed questionnaire administration. The questionnaire and consequent profiles were thus continuously tested against a rich context of whole-child information and feedback.

With the opportunity offered by this 4–16 development, it was decided to base the new matrix primarily upon this continuously evolving version. One significant difference between this matrix and its predecessors is that the questions, responses and the resulting profiles and reports have been recalibrated to describe **strengths** as well as **difficulties** and so, while the primary purpose is to identify areas and skills a pupil needs to develop and to provide guidance about how best to do so, it also allows users to talk to teachers, pupils and families about each pupil's patterns of distinctive strengths. The pupil's own voice, too, is given much greater attention.

Traditional cross-validation of assessment instruments relies upon comparing the outcomes of one instrument against others that explore similar skills, traits and qualities and to seek an appropriate level of congruence. For SNAP-SpLD, this has not been possible, as there are no other instruments with the same scope, intentions or methodology. From the start of Version 1, SNAP has been seen as a 'research instrument', in a condition of continuing evolution, and its validity can only be tested or assessed through a process of continuous comparison with the reality of a pupil's learning and his or her development as a learner. Using this criterion, it is felt that there is a high level of validity. The development of SNAP-SpLD has depended uniquely upon this cycle of development / feedback / adjustment / further feedback, and it should continue to do so.

However, for this version, while the absence of any directly parallel instrument precluded any precise cross-validation, it was felt that some more holistic cross-validation would be useful and appropriate. Accordingly, three case studies were conducted where the pupil was assessed using SNAP-SpLD 4–16 as well as undertaking full assessment by an educational psychologist (one of the authors). The aim was to compare the overall conclusions and general profiles revealed by each assessment method. The outcomes are reported below.

The perceived need for SNAP-SpLD

The potential sources of confusion when seeking to identify a pupil's SpLD are discussed in Chapter 1, as is the potential complexity of the interacting factors from which any individual pupil's SpLD profile may emerge. All those working with learning difficulties are aware of this complexity. We are aware, too, that even the best of our responses sometimes seem too simplistic: there is a nagging and lingering sense of important issues that perhaps remain unaddressed.

In seeking to gain an overview of such a complex situation, traditional psychometrics offer only part of the answer. By definition, an effective psychometric test has to be precisely focused – its validity and reliability depend on its precision. But precision of focus is part of our problem, as well as part of our solution: by focusing closely on a predetermined skill we may miss adjacent but important skills. For a pupil with SpLD, it is this shadow that we need probe and clarify.

It does not seem feasible to derive and apply standardised tests which answer all the questions that arise (although the SNAP-SpLD probes do allow quite extensive quantitative insight). And perhaps it is not necessary to try to develop such an instrument, as there are other diagnostic models that are widely used. Medical diagnosticians and clinical psychologists, for example, may draw upon some quantitative information but it will be used in conjunction with clinical judgements that are informed by comprehensive and consensually agreed diagnostic checklists.

Therefore, this was the intention informing the development of SNAP-SpLD – to access and organise all that is already known about a pupil in a way that allows comparison with consensually agreed checklists, supported by quantitative data but not primarily dependent upon it.

The development process

The principle underlying the package is simple: questions are asked of those who know the pupil and these are supplemented if necessary by information from the Diagnostic Probes (significantly enhanced and more heavily weighted in SNAP-SpLD 4–16). These questions derive directly from the checklists of presenting characteristics for each SpLD and condition, so that the information gained about each pupil maps directly onto a matrix of SpLDs and conditions. This allows an indication of the extent to which each difficulty appears to be present for each pupil.

The original development process comprised several main stages; each one is also reflected in developing the current version:

- defining the terms and concepts
- identifying the SpLDs and conditions to be included
- achieving consensus over checklists of presenting characteristics for each SpLD and condition
- developing the questions and the underlying matrix
- trialling and refining the questions and the matrix
- developing and trialling the Diagnostic Probes.

Defining the terms and concepts

By 'specific learning difficulties', we mean a weakness in a pupil's performance in a specific skill area in relation to that pupil's general level of performance. It is a relative weakness that, if unaddressed and uncorrected, is likely to prevent that pupil from reaching his or her educational potential. The idea of discrepancy is central. A dictionary tells us that something that is specific is 'precise' and 'distinct' – that is, something which stands out in contrast to its background. Implicit in the very phrase, then, is a contrast with more global, or general, learning difficulties.

In a model of multiple intelligences, a specific difficulty would be a low level of functioning in one (or more) intelligences, in contrast to a generally higher level of function across the other intelligences. A global difficulty would imply a low level of functioning across the range of intelligences.

Identifying the SpLDs and conditions to be included

To chart the strands that might comprise an individual's SpLD profile, a decision had to be reached about which SpLDs should be included. 'Separability' was a key concept in arriving at this decision. For example, phonological difficulties and literacy difficulties are very frequently accompanied by working memory difficulties and information processing difficulties – combined, they comprise key features of developmental phonological dyslexia, so arguably they might be combined as a single SpLD rather than as four separate SpLDs. But, because each of these four strands may sometimes be encountered in isolation or in different combinations, each of them has to be regarded as a separate element. Therefore, there is a presumption of potential independence for each of these SpLDs and conditions: each, it is suggested, could appear in isolation but is far more likely to appear in combination with at least one other.

The SpLDs and conditions finally chosen do not in any way form a comprehensive listing. They emerged from:

- the assessment and SpLD literature
- the assessment experience of the authors
- scrutiny of assessment reports from educational psychologists across the English-speaking world
- peer scrutiny and comment
- scrutiny from other relevant professionals – academic psychologists, a paediatrician and a paediatric neuro-psychologist
- the iterative process of matrix development described above.

Scrutiny from peers and other professionals was particularly helpful, and their contributions were usually reflected in progressive changes to the list of SpLDs. In taking their comments into account, a balance had to be found between 'hard science' and the lure of approaches that are still generally regarded as 'alternative', for which a rigorous evidential base has not yet emerged (and may not!), but which nonetheless inform the practice of many of those involved in assessing and responding to SpLDs.

The list could have been far longer, including other difficulties (e.g. Semantic Pragmatic Disorder or Oppositional Defiant Disorder) or subdividing some of the SpLDs (e.g. dysgraphia could be subdivided into dyspraxic dysgraphia, phonological dysgraphia and visuo-spatial dysgraphia). Prototype versions of SNAP included up to 31 SpLDs and conditions; the current iteration emerged from consideration of the sources listed above together with the level of detail that would be valuable and practical for the school-based practitioner.

The changes with each successive version of SNAP (from Version 1 through 2 and 2.5 to 3, and now SNAP-SpLD 4–16) have centred on developing insights into the nature of the barriers that learners face and also on our accumulating experience with this instrument. For example, at different iterations 'Information Processing' divided into 'Processing Speed' and 'Auditory Processing'; 'Self-esteem' was introduced; 'Involuntary Speech and Motor Difficulties' were included and then omitted; 'Fatty Acid Deficiency' has been omitted; 'Working Memory' has been sub-divided to offer separate insights into auditory and visual working memory; and others of the strands were amended, regrouped or reconceptualised to a greater or lesser extent. At each stage, questions and weightings were amended while some questions were omitted and new questions were added in the light of emerging experience. The emerging instrument was reviewed and critiqued by paediatricians and paediatric neuro-psychologists, and again adjusted in light of this.

Despite our best attempts, and probably inevitably, the 22 SpLDs and conditions in Version 3, the 13 in the renewed 4–6 matrix and the 18 in the renewed 7–16 matrix still overlapped in many places (the two self-esteem strands excluded). It did not then, and does not now, seem helpful or feasible to try to organise them hierarchically or along a continuum from 'cause' to 'effect' – although it is evident that there are such relationships between them. For example, a 'Literacy Difficulty' may be the result of a

'Visual Processing Difficulty', but it is less likely to be the cause of it. Even this, though, may not always be the case: poor visual tracking may make reading hard; but it may result, too, from a lack of the kind of regular left/right eye movement that is arguably unique to skilled reading of Western alphabets. Similarly, it is entirely possible that a 'Working Memory Difficulty' may be caused by 'Information Processing Difficulties' and that both of these might stem from an 'Attention Difficulty'.

Developing the questions and the underlying matrix

Having agreed on the presenting features for each SpLD and condition, each was then phrased as a question and entered onto the matrix of scores and weightings. The questions were organised into coherent domains to allow the user to focus upon particular aspects of the pupil at one time.

In this version for the 4–6 years' matrix, the domains are:

- speech and language: talking
- speech and language: listening
- literacy and numeracy
- personal
- play and coordination
- behaviour and relationships with others
- information from the Family Questionnaire.

In this version for the 7–16 years' matrix, the domains are:

- reading
- spelling
- writing
- maths and number
- speech and language
- general schoolwork
- personal characteristics
- behaviour with others
- movement, balance and coordination
- attention
- level of activity
- information from the Family Questionnaire.

Trialling and refining the questions and matrix

The draft matrix and questions were refined through a sequence of trials, some with pupils with known and documented learning difficulties and some with pupils being assessed for the first time.

Feedback from this trialling allowed a process of continuing refinement and development in terms of validity, phrasing, user-friendliness, the optimum number of response options, and refining the weightings and formulae underpinning the equations in the underlying matrix. This process of refining/developing continues with each subsequent version of the assessment.

Developing the Diagnostic Probes

A small number of the questions could clearly not always be answered on the basis of observation and existing knowledge, and so supplementary Diagnostic Probes were developed for each of these. For this version, these have been reduced in number but have been given a significantly increased weighting and an enhanced role in the instrument overall.

The development of the original probes ran in parallel with the development and refinement of the main matrix. It was decided to call them 'probes' rather than 'tests' specifically to reduce user expectations of their precision. Each one provides no more than an approximate clinical insight – they do not aim to rank or make fine discriminations between levels of performance and have not been piloted and standardised in a way that would allow this. Instead, they offer an approximate insight into which category a pupil's scores/performance falls. For most of the probes, in terms of an assumed normal distribution, this equates to quintile ranges for percentiles:

- well above average
- above average
- age appropriate
- below average
- well below average

- 0–20%
- 21–40%
- 41–60%
- 61–80%
- 81–100%

For three of the probes (Balance, Visual Memory and Picture Naming) it was felt that the data obtained during the Version 3 trialling appeared more robust and potentially valid than that gathered later, and this data was used for deriving the norms. This means that, for these three probes, a child's performance is allocated to one of three categories rather than five – Above average, Average, Below average.

The sample was a stratified, opportunity sample, with a sample size of 120. Participating schools were asked to test 3 categories of pupils from each year group: those deemed to be coping easily with academic demands; those coping adequately at an average level; and those who find the demands of the curriculum quite challenging.

Formal test construction procedures were not applied in full, and this needs to be remembered when considering probe scores. For three of the probes the data set was insufficiently comprehensive (hence the use of Version 3 trial data for three of the probes). Any questionable data was edited out (e.g. where the test administrator had not apparently understood the instructions and entered a score outside the range), and quintiles then derived. These were plotted as line graphs across the age range and a line of best fit applied to each. These lines of best fit were then used to allocate scores to categories of response for each age.

Clearly, norm derivation for these probes drew upon a significant level of professional judgement to support and interpret the raw data. It must be emphasised that these are *not* standardised tests in the usual sense of the word – they probe a skill sufficiently to allow an approximate insight but no more. While they provide valuable insight, they must not be seen as standardised test scores – far more extensive standardisation trials would have been needed for this.

Although such arrangements would not be adequate for the development of a full psychometric test, it is felt that they were more than sufficient for these purposes. The cross-validation studies confirmed this – the probe norms provided an unexpectedly accurate reflection of the skill sets identified by the standardised tests used in the educational psychologist assessments.

Cross-validation studies

Three cross-validation studies were completed. For each, two assessments of the child were carried out: one using the SNAP-SpLD package, and the other an educational psychologist assessment using primarily the WIAT-2 and WISC-IV batteries.

For each study, the conclusions and recommendations from each assessment are set out, followed by a brief comparative comment.

Pupil A Female age 7 years 4 months

Conclusions and recommendations taken from Pupil A's educational psychologist assessment report

> 'Data from this assessment suggest an intelligent girl whose literacy is developing very much less swiftly and automatically than would be predicted from her level of overall cognitive function.
>
> There is, then, a clearly defined and significant **dyslexic** difficulty – and while at this stage such labels have only limited value, they may be valuable later as a means of accessing special examination arrangements, in the event that any are needed, as well as allowing a learner to understand why she is finding some aspects of school relatively hard.
>
> It is a very characteristic dyslexic profile – as well as literacy scores that lag consistently and significantly behind the levels that would be expected, her cognitive profile is very typical of such difficulties, with low indices for auditory working memory and processing speed.'

From Pupil A's SNAP-SpLD assessment

Core Profile

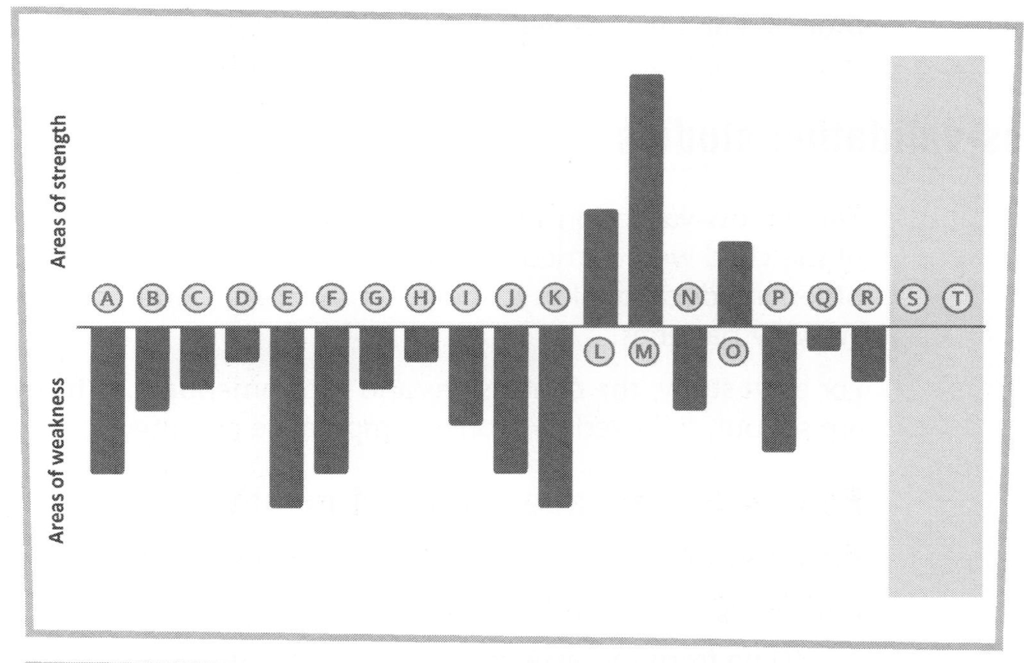

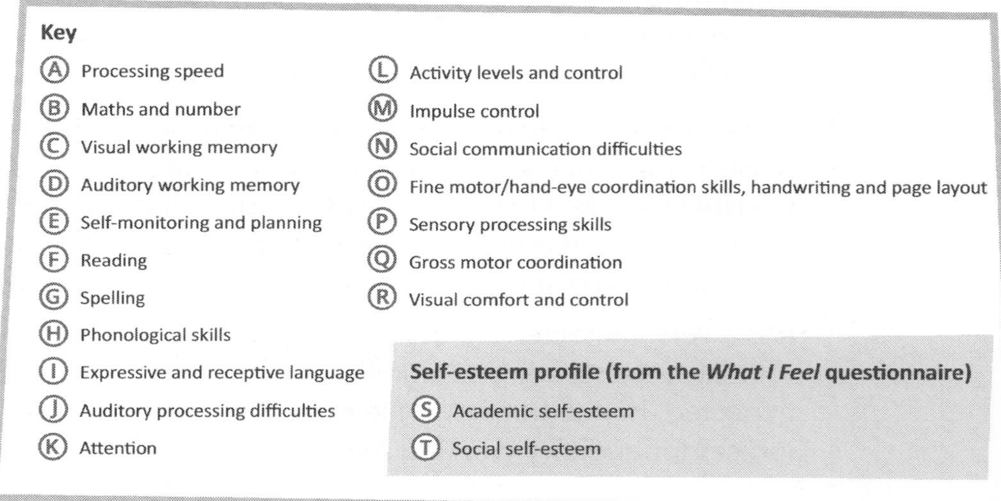

The questionnaire responses suggested a calm and self-controlled girl, but one whose ability to sustain attention is still relatively weak, who finds it hard to multi-task and whose reading is an area of real weakness.

Pupil A's probe scores suggest very good listening skills but great difficulty in reading for understanding (see Figure 7.1) – her understanding was significantly stronger when listening than when reading. She clearly has no difficulty in understanding the ideas being conveyed by text when she is reading – her difficulty is wholly with the mechanics of decoding the text.

The pupil's scores were very low too on all aspects of phonological processing (sound deletion and non-word reading), as was her spelling score. Her scores for speed and quality of writing (timed text copying) were well below average, as was her speed of word access and retrieval (picture naming).

Pupil A's memory, both visual and auditory, were good, as was her balance.

1A Reading	0 = well below
1B Listening	7 = well above
2A Sound deletion	3 = well below
2B Non-words	11 = well below
3 Spelling	5 = well below
4 Timed text copying	8 = well below
5 Backward span	5 = above
6 Visual memory	10 = above
7 Balance	9 = above
8 Picture naming	103 = below

Figure 7.1: Pupil A's probe scores

Comment

There is just one apparent discrepancy: the auditory memory score from the educational psychologist assessment suggests a relative *weakness*, while the Backward Span probe from SNAP-SpLD suggests a modest *strength* in auditory memory. However, the assessment approach in the two batteries is slightly different: the former battery tests auditory memory by asking the child to repeat a list of digits, while the SNAP probe asks him or her to repeat the names of objects. It seems likely that Pupil A used her strong visual memory to retain the items in mind, something she would be less able to do with digits.

Overall, the two assessments are generally highly congruent, both highlighting literacy difficulties of a dyslexic nature. The SNAP-SpLD assessment provides further and significant insight into the contrast between Pupil A's high level of impulse control and low level of attentional skills and self-monitoring and planning.

Pupil B Female age 8 years 4 months

Conclusions and recommendations taken from Pupil B's educational psychologist assessment report

> 'Evidence from this assessment suggests an intelligent girl with some unusual cognitive strengths, some modest cognitive/perceptual weaknesses that are very characteristic of dyslexic difficulties (working memory and processing speed), and literacy that is lagging very significantly behind the level that would be predicted from her level of intellectual function.
>
> To this extent, then, there is a clearly defined and significant specific learning difficulty that would be described as **dyslexic** in nature – and while at this stage such labels have only limited value, they may be valuable later as a means of accessing special examination arrangements, in the event that any are needed, as well as allowing the learner to understand why she is finding some aspects of school relatively hard.'

From Pupil B's SNAP-SpLD assessment

Core Profile

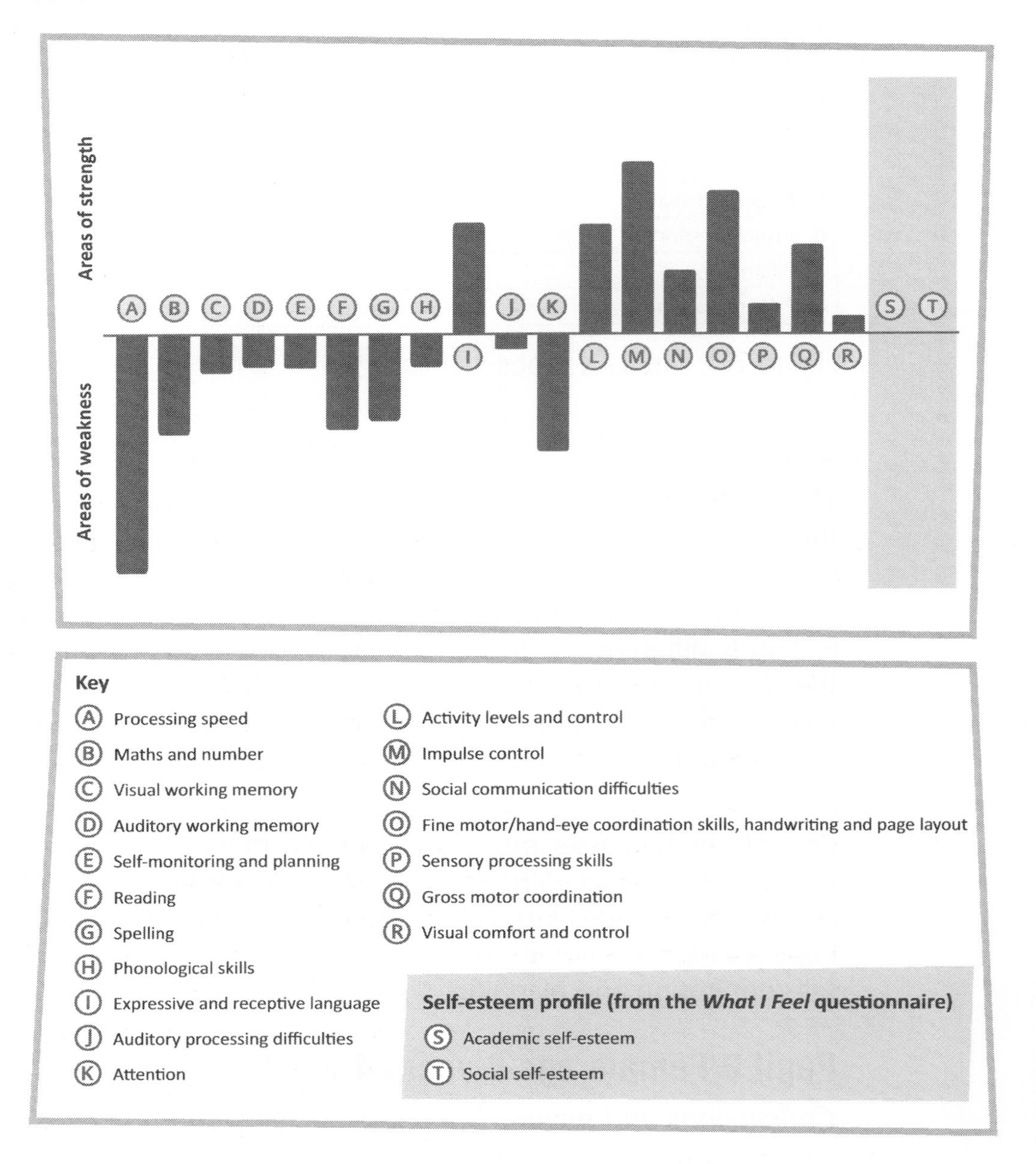

The questionnaire responses suggested a very significant difficulty with speed of processing, and more modest difficulties with number, reading and spelling, and sustaining attention. It suggested well developed language skills, coordination (both fine and gross), and a well developed ability to manage her own impulses.

Pupil B's probe scores (see Figure 7.2) confirm excellent listening but very much weaker reading for understanding. Visual issues and use of yellow overlay discussed in the educational psychologist report are reflected here, in that her phonological skills in the sound deletion task are competent, above average, while her reading of non-words is much weaker – the evidence suggests that her dyslexia may be more visual than phonological in nature. Her spelling score is well below average; her picture naming in both analyses is weak. Her balance is good, congruent with the good coordination noted in the educational psychologist analysis.

The pupil's working memory in average range in SNAP-SpLD, but at lower end of the average range, and is at the lower end of the average range in the WISC profile. It is a relative weakness for Pupil B, not an absolute one.

1A Reading	4 = below
1B Listening	8 = well above
2 Sound deletion	9 = above
2 non-words	11 = well below
3 Spelling	6 = well below
4 Timed text copying	10 = below
5 Backward span	3 = average
6 Visual memory	3 = below
7 Balance	7 = above
8 Picture naming	82 = below

Figure 7.2: Pupil B's probe scores

Comment

The two assessments are highly congruent, both highlighting similar literacy difficulties of a dyslexic nature.

Pupil C Female age 14 years 5 months

Conclusions and recommendations taken from Pupil C's educational psychologist assessment report

'Data from this assessment suggests an intelligent, thoughtful and competent girl, and one for whom all the core academic skills needed for learning appear to be in place and well developed. There appear to be no obvious cognitive or academic reasons why she should not cope well within the curriculum.

The only areas of modest weakness in the profile derived from the formal testing are perhaps identified by her relative difficulty in the Coding task, where her speed of copying small abstract symbols was a little lower than would be expected. As discussed, this is often linked to poor handwriting and slow writing – but this does not appear to be the case for [Pupil C]. Her handwriting is swift and legible, and the only indication of any possible issue is that her script is non-cursive, but this does not appear to be incapacitating her.

However, she clearly does find some aspects of the classroom and the curriculum difficult and to some extent daunting, and it is both tempting and arguably plausible to attribute this at least in part to her sensory sensitivities, the hyperacusis or misophonia. It seems entirely likely that any attention difficulties derive directly from these hearing issues – as she demonstrated in the assessment tasks she can be impressively attentive and tenacious, holding information in mind over a prolonged period and returning to it to work with it; but as she also demonstrated her attention can be all-too-easily derailed, by distractions and noises that appear to others to be insignificant.'

From Pupil C's SNAP-SpLD assessment

Core Profile

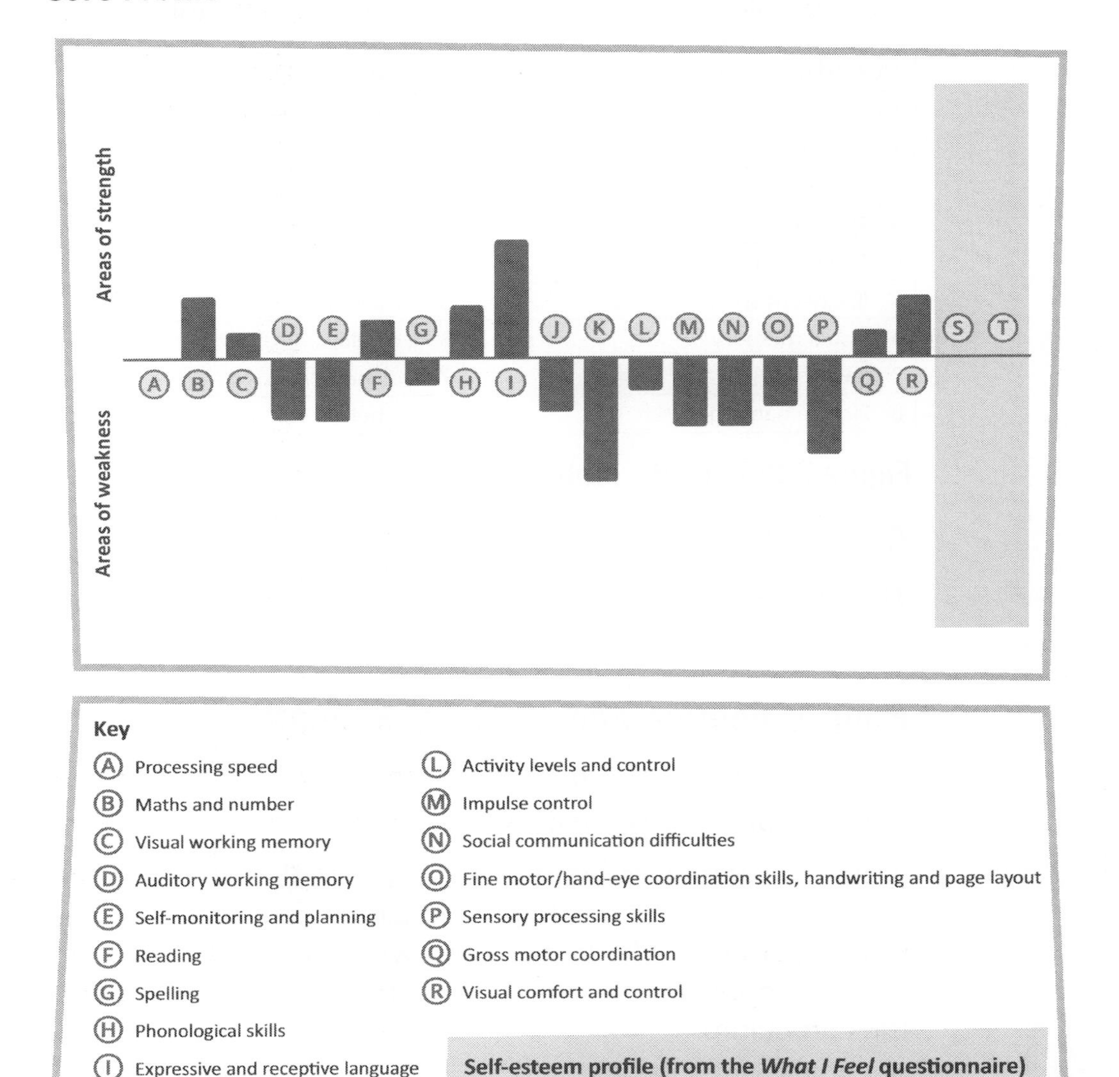

The questionnaire responses suggested significant attentional difficulties, and clearly defined issues with sensory sensitivities and with impulse control. A number of other areas, while in the average range for Pupil C's age, were consistently rather below that average – auditory working memory, self-monitoring and planning, auditory processing, and sensory integration and sensitivities. Reading and spelling were approximately at the expected levels for her age. Her expressive and receptive language skills were an area of clearly defined strength, and her number appears to be at least adequately established.

It is not a profile pattern that suggests any significant specific learning difficulties, despite the difficulties with attention and sensory sensitivities.

Pupil C's probe scores (see Figure 7.3) suggest good reading and spelling, and good listening, exactly as indicated in the educational psychologist report. Her SNAP-SpLD rapid naming score was at the lower end of the average range, as it was in the educational psychologist profile. Writing speed was good in each assessment; her auditory memory was above average in SNAP-SpLD and in the WISC Digit Span.

1A Reading	12 = well above
1B Listening	13 = well above
2 Sound deletion	10 = average or above
2 non-words	28 = well above
3 Spelling	19 = well above
4 Timed text copying	26 = above
5 Backward span	8 = above
6 Visual memory	10 = average or above
7 Balance	0 = below
8 Picture naming	36 = average

Figure 7.3: Pupil C's probe scores

Comment

The two assessments are highly congruent, both recognising poor attentional skills and sensory sensitivities while confirming that there appear to be no specific learning difficulties, and that Pupil C appears adequately equipped with the core academic skills needed to cope in the classroom.